EYES ₒ𝒻 ᴛʜᴇ HEART

"Opening Christine Paintner's *Eyes of the Heart* is like entering a garden in full bloom. It opens up all your senses so you see, smell, taste, and touch the world in a whole new way. Paintner has a gift for reuniting the transcendent and the immanent. She calls God home. She sees the Divine in the pebble on the path, hears its sound in the buzzing mosquito. This modern-day monk knows the essential secrets to sacred living and joyful being and she shares them freely."

Jan Phillips
Author of *No Ordinary Time*

"Christine Valters Paintner explores the eye as a window to the heart. Using scripture and observations from thinkers in all faiths she offers a spirituality of photography as writing with light. This monk, photographer-artist, and writer combines the art of image receiving with visio divina, taking us through a detailed program for the feeling, reflecting, and completion of our heart's vision."

Brother John J. O'Hara, S.A.
Graymoor Spiritual Life Center

"*Eyes of the Heart* is more than a celebration of God's presence in the world. It is itself an experience of receiving the Divine directly within. Paintner's insights and exercises lead the reader to a personal, intimate encounter with divinity. In the process, she also illuminates the way to self-understanding and creative serenity."

Anthony F. Chiffolo
Author of *100 Names of Mary*

PHOTOGRAPHY AS A CHRISTIAN CONTEMPLATIVE PRACTICE

EYES OF THE HEART

CHRISTINE VALTERS PAINTNER | author of *The Artist's Rule*

Sorin Books Notre Dame, Indiana

Permissions:

Carole Satyamurti, *Stitching the Dark: New & Selected Poems* (Bloodaxe Books, 2005). Used with permission.

Joanna Paterson, "This Is Not Photography," Joannapaterson.co.uk (accessed on September 12, 2012).

© 2013 by Christine Valters Paintner

www.sorinbooks.com

Paperback: ISBN-10 1-933495-54-5, ISBN-13 978-1933495-54-5

E-book: ISBN-10 1-933495-55-3, ISBN-13 978-1933495-55-2

Cover image and interior photography © Christine Valters Paintner.

Cover and text design by Brian C. Conley.

Printed and bound in the United States of America.

Library of Congress Cataloging-in-Publication Data
Paintner, Christine Valters.
   Eyes of the heart : photography as a Christian contemplative practice / Christine Valters Paintner.
       p. cm.
   ISBN 978-1-933495-54-5 (pbk.) -- ISBN 1-933495-54-5 (pbk.)
   1. Photography--Religious aspects--Christianity. 2. Contemplation. 3. Spiritual life--Christianity. I. Title.
   BR115.A8P35 2013
   248.3'4--dc23
                          2012039722

To my grandparents Faith and Fred Fitts, who helped to instill in me a very early appreciation for the gifts of photography.

CONTENTS

Introduction **1**

1. Seeing with Eyes of the Heart **11**

2. Practices and Tools to Cultivate Vision **29**

3. The Dance of Light and Shadow **41**

4. What Is Hidden and What Is Revealed? **57**

5. The Symbolic Significance of Color **77**

6. What Is Mirrored Back? **91**

7. Discovering the Holy within Us **105**

8. Seeing the Holy Everywhere **121**

Conclusion **133**

Acknowledgments **137**

Notes **139**

Additional Resources **143**

INTRODUCTION

May the eyes of your hearts be enlightened.

—Ephesians 1:18

By virtue of the Creation and, still more, of the Incarnation,
nothing here below is profane for those who know how to
see.

—Pierre Teilhard de Chardin

My journey with photography began when I was a very young girl.
My maternal grandparents owned a chain of photography stores
called Fitts Photo & Hobby Shop in Massachusetts, Vermont, and
New Hampshire, and so I have owned a camera for as long as I can
remember.

Photography has always been a way for me to see more deeply,
but my awareness of how this was an experience of prayer and often
an encounter with the sacred presence emerged over time. It wasn't
until I embraced monastic spirituality in my late twenties that I began to experience photography consciously as a contemplative practice. I made a commitment as a Benedictine oblate at St. Placid Priory
to deepen my own contemplative path. I began to see photography
as a way to slow down and gaze deeply, noticing things I missed in

my rushed life. For me, the camera provided an encounter with the eternal moment—that place in which I was able to suddenly become so present to what I was gazing upon that I lost track of time, allowing eternity to break in. It became a tool for deeper vision, supporting and enlivening contemplative seeing.

As my work began to take contemplative form, I began publishing my photos on my website AbbeyoftheArts.com in a prayerful and reflective context, as an adjunct to my writing. A global, online monastery, the website is dedicated to the integration of contemplative practice and creative expression. And in inviting others into contemplative space with me visually, I have been able to ask people to pause on a particular moment in time and see an aspect of the holy revealed in that image.

This book emerges from that holy seeing and from three of the identities I hold: monk in the world, photographer-artist, and writer. The way of the monk and the path of the artist together have been essential nourishment for my own spiritual deepening. My commitment to contemplative rhythms with slow, spacious attentiveness, and to creative expression by following what brings me alive, is an integration of practice that speaks most to my soul.

One of my previous books with Ave Maria Press, *The Artist's Rule: Nurturing Your Creative Soul with Monastic Wisdom*, builds on this process of integrating the contemplative and creative—as do the classes I teach on contemplative photography. *Eyes of the Heart* takes that process into direct expression and combination, moving from ideas and principles to specific explorations, of spirituality and the lens of our eyes, the lens of the camera. Photography is often seen as a tool to be used for far-flung journeys and recording family events, but a photographic journey can also be taken right in your own neighborhood—as close as the block you live on—as a way of discovering in new ways the everyday places you inhabit. With a special camera, or with a cell phone camera, a photograph can be made special by your discovery, by paying attention. One of the gifts of phones with built-in cameras, and places for sharing like Facebook and Twitter, is that we are encouraged to make this kind of creative expression a daily event and practice.

Photography as a spiritual practice combines the active art of image-receiving with the contemplative nature and open-heartedness of prayer. It cultivates what I call sacred seeing or seeing with the "eyes of the heart" (Ephesians 1:18). This kind of seeing is our ability to receive the world around us at a deeper level than surface realities.

We live in a product-oriented culture, where much of what we do is focused on an end goal or product to share. When we approach art in this way, we become distracted by trying to produce a beautiful image. When we focus on the *process* of art-making, rather than the *product,* we can immerse ourselves in the creative journey and discover the ways God is moving through our lives and how we are being invited to respond. We release our own plans and expectations and pay attention to what is actually unfolding within us.

The process of art-making or prayer becomes a journey of discovery, where we open ourselves to what is being revealed moment by moment, rather than what we hope or expect to see. This book offers an invitation to transform photography into a spiritual practice by attending to the process, and thereby deepening our relationship to God, to the world around us, and to ourselves.

Mythologist and storyteller Michael Meade says the word "moment" comes from the Latin root *momentus,* which means to move. We are moved when we touch the eternal and timeless. There is a sense of spaciousness in moments. We linger and feel lifted above the daily concerns of *chronos* time and dwell in *kairos* time. Both of these words come from Greek and help us differentiate the different qualities of time we experience. *Chronos* time is the sequential time of schedules and moving through the tasks of everyday life, the time we are aware of when we watch the clock waiting for the workday to be done. *Kairos* time has an altogether different quality. It is not sequential or linear. *Kairos* refers to the fullness of a given moment, a moment when something special happens, something unexpected. We can never plan *kairos* time, but we can make ourselves available to being seized by it through cultivating contemplative practice.

Giving ourselves over to the act of art-making is one way we find this moment of eternity, or even better, *how we allow the moment to find us*. There are *many* moments waiting for us each day, prodding at our consciousness, inviting us to abandon our carefully constructed plans and defenses and open our hearts to what is before us. The task of the artist is to cultivate the ability to see these eternal moments again and again. In this way, we are all invited to become artists.

For me, *both* art and spirituality are truly about tending to the moments of life: listening deeply, holding space, encountering the sacred, and touching eternity. For a few seconds I touch time beyond time, and in that spacious presence my heart grows wider, my imagination frees, my breath catches, and I am held in awe and wonder. These are the moments that help to make life full of meaning.

We know we have touched this moment when we are moved by something beyond us yet also rising from deep within. We may be moved to tears or to laughter, or maybe both. In these moments, the particulars of the world open us up to a great expanse. We suddenly see the other world hidden in the heart of this one. We may not know exactly why or how, but we know we have been touched and transformed, invited into greater compassion for ourselves and the world.

One of the great metaphors we find across spiritual traditions for our deepening life in God is that of awakening. In the Gospel of Mark 13:33–37, Jesus commands his disciples to "keep awake" three times in a single passage. The Sufi poet Rumi writes, "The breezes at dawn have secrets to tell you / don't go back to sleep."

This chorus of wakefulness is not about sleep deprivation but about resisting our human urge to fall asleep to life, to numb ourselves through excessive time spent online, watching television, overeating, drinking too much, addiction to drugs, workaholism, or anything that distracts us from what is most real. Most meditation practices are, at heart, about staying awake to life, being fully present to our experience, and becoming aware of our own preconceived ideas and expectations that obscure our vision.

The slumber of being human creates a veil between our eyes and the truth of the world around us. Photography as a spiritual practice can help us to cultivate an awakened vision so we begin to really see. Contemplative art can express and embody the "awake" state of being discovered in meditation practice.

The contemplative practice of photography has an especial depth. I take my camera out into the world, and it invites me to slow down and linger over these moments of beauty. It opens me to wonder and delight. As I cultivate sacred seeing, I grow my ability to see the world beneath the surface appearance of things.

There is a quote I love from the film *Waking Life* about movies that applies to photography as well:

> Film is a record of the ever-changing face of God. This moment is holy, but we walk around like it's not holy. We walk around like there are some holy moments and there are all the other moments that are not holy. [But they are,] and film can let us see that. Film can frame it so we can see that, Ah! This moment. Holy.

For me, this is one of the wonders of photography: to be able to frame a moment in time and, within my gaze and absolute presence in that particular moment, to discover holiness. In that single moment, I am reminded that all moments are holy.

Photography is an ideal prayer practice for those who desire more active forms of contemplation or want to integrate creative expression into their spiritual path. Because photography is so accessible and basic equipment very affordable, anyone can take photos. Fancy or expensive equipment is not required, just a digital camera, a smartphone or iPhone camera, or even a disposable model camera or Lomo will do, along with a journal and pen for written reflection.

Consider carrying these basic tools with you in your bag at all times, so that you begin to cultivate an understanding of yourself as an artist of everyday life and a monk in the world, one who slows down and really sees at all times. As the Best Camera website philosophy goes, "The best camera is the one that's with you."

Essentially this is a book about seeing, about cultivating a deeper kind of vision, rather than a kind of technical manual on photography. The camera is simply the tool to support this; that vision is about seeing more deeply in all of life. While this isn't a manual, this book will draw on the language of photography—light and shadow, framing, use of color, reflections—in order to see differently, to offer an invitation to our spiritual eyes as well, as light and framing become metaphors for our inner life.

Photography can be an act of silent worship. When we see the world with eyes of the heart, we can engage in an act of both reverence and self-expression. We can discover how the living Spirit is being revealed in the world. This book combines an inward vision with an outward expression and through a creative act helps us both discover and celebrate our spiritual path.

While you don't need to be a photographer to engage in this book, my hope is that you feel energized and passionate about the camera lens as a metaphor for spiritual seeing—and that you are willing to take risks and stretch yourself in order to expand your vision.

Overview of the Chapters

Throughout the book, we will explore different aspects of the art of photography as a metaphor for the spiritual journey. Chapter 1 lays the groundwork for the spiritual journey, exploring what it means to see with the "eyes of the heart." In chapter 2, we will be invited to take our camera out into the world for photographic journeys and meet a form of lectio divina called "visio divina," or sacred seeing.

Essentially we take the four movements of this ancient contemplative practice of lectio, and instead of praying with scripture, we bring our gaze to the world around us as sacred text. This practice focuses us on *receiving images*, rather than *taking* or *making* images.

Chapter 3 explores the play of light and dark, illumination and shadow, much as the spiritual journey is a practice of paying attention to these elements of our own lives and how we meet the holy revealed in each. Chapter 4 examines the choices we make in the visual framing of elements, what to include and what to exclude, whether we zoom in or pull back. This is a practice of visual discernment: a way of choosing what is important and what needs to be let go of, a practice that can also inform our personal discernment. In chapter 5 we explore the significance and impact of color, and the impact color makes on us both visually within a photograph and as a metaphor for the spiritual life. Chapter 6 invites you to consider the mirror as a place of reflection, seeing what you discover when you look at things through another perspective. Chapter 7 explores self-portraits and how this self-exploration might reveal unclaimed beauty. Chapter 8 asks you to engage photography as a way of opening explicitly to a variety of images of God.

While I have taken many workshops over the last several years on the craft of photography and other visual arts, my main training in the arts comes from the field of expressive arts, primarily focusing on art as a process of *healing and transformation*. Through this lens, the arts become a place of discovery. Each chapter, then, is framed and informed by this process. This book is about cultivating your ability to see with, what St. Paul describes in his letter to the Ephesians, the "eyes of the heart" (1:18). The camera is merely a tool for practice.

An Overview of the Format

The format of each chapter includes various reflections on the theme we are exploring from both spiritual and photographic perspectives. Working with the language of photography helps us to break open our inner journey in new ways, so the more we grow intimate with the tools of the camera, or even the basic tools of the smartphone camera, the more they can serve our own deepening spiritual journey.

Following the chapter reflections is a meditation experience. You can either move through it by reading and pausing to imagine what is suggested, or you could record your voice speaking the meditation aloud to listen to later and move you through the experience. The purpose of the meditation is to give you another entry point to the theme, having a felt and sensory experience, rather than merely reading and thinking about a chapter theme.

Included also are photographic explorations. In these explorations, we bring our camera out into the world for a contemplative walk and pay attention to images that are being offered to us in connection with the chapter's theme. Each photographic exploration provides an accompanying photo, my own example of that particular photographic exploration.

Finally, each chapter concludes with suggested questions for reflection, allowing you to engage with the material in an ongoing way.

I encourage you to enter into the experience of visio divina as a prayer, a communion with your Creative Source, and see if you can release any worries about making a beautiful product. As an authentic expression of your longings and unique soul, it will inevitably have its own beauty. There is certainly a place for the role of craft and fine art in photography. But our focus here in this book is on allowing your authentic expression as a response to being fully present to the world around you to come through as much as possible.

How to Engage in This Book

This book is process oriented. That means it's not meant to be consumed in one sitting but rather practiced and integrated over time. Consider reading one chapter each week and making time during the week to engage in that chapter's explorations. See what you begin to notice about the way you are seeing the world even when you don't have a camera in your hand.

You might also consider working through this material with a small group, meeting once a week or once a month to share your reflections and images together.

Additional resources on engaging in the contemplative and artistic life are available on my website AbbeyoftheArts.com, along with options for a guided online class experience in conjunction with this process.

Let us begin the journey.

1

SEEING WITH EYES OF THE HEART

Description is revelation. Seeing is praise.

—**Chet Raymo**

The real voyage of discovery consists not in seeking new
landscapes but in having new eyes.

—**Marcel Proust**

You were within me, and I was outside, and it was there
I searched for you. . . . On entering into myself I saw, as it
were with the eyes of my soul, what was beyond the eyes of
the soul, beyond my spirit: your immutable light.

—**St. Augustine**

The Spiritual Senses

There is a long mystical tradition of understanding that our five physical senses of taste, touch, sight, smell, and hearing have five paral-
lel mystical senses that operate in similar ways. Just as our physical
senses help us to perceive and encounter the world, so our mystical or spiritual senses help us to perceive and encounter God. The

spiritual journey is, in part, about awakening these capacities and cultivating them. Sense here refers to a faculty of spiritual perception or experience. These spiritual senses are subject to decreased capacity because of our human limitations but can be cultivated through practice and grace. Part of the spiritual journey is learning how to see, not with our physical eyes, but with our spiritual eyes. Spiritual seeing simply receives the present moment without judgment or trying to make plans or set agendas, which is a lot more challenging for most of us than it might sound.

The third-century church father Origen was the first to develop this idea of the spiritual senses, which is rooted in scripture. Origen writes, "After thorough investigation one can say that there exists, according to the word of Scripture, a general sense or faculty for the divine. Only the blessed know how to find it, as we read in the Wisdom of Solomon, 'You discover the divine faculty of perception' (Proverbs 2:5)." He describes how the spiritual sense unfolds:

> This sense, however, unfolds, in various individual faculties: sight for the contemplation of immaterial forms, as is evidently granted in the Cherubim and Seraphim, hearing for the discrimination of voices, which do not echo in the empty air, taste in order to savour the living bread which came down from heaven to bring life to the world (John 6:33), and even a sense of smell, with which Paul perceived those realities which caused him to describe himself as a sweet odour of Christ (2 Corinthians 2:15), and finally touch, which possessed John when he states that he has touched with his own hands the Word of life (1 John 1:1).[1]

In the gospels, blindness is used as a metaphor for being unable to see truth. St. Augustine wrestles with this idea in his book *City of God*, where he describes the vision we are to have one day—*visio dei*, or the clear sight of God. In the book of Exodus (33:18–23), even Moses who comes face to face with God when asked to see God's glory is granted only a glimpse of God's backside. Our human capacity to perceive is limited because God's full glory is too radiant for us to bear fully.

Yet the graced eye can glimpse beauty everywhere, seeing the divine at work in the hidden depths of things. It is so easy to let our senses be dulled and to settle for the ordinary. Often, life seems to be just what it offers on the surface; as Ecclesiastes puts it, "there is nothing new under the sun" (1:9). The technology, speed, and busyness so prized by our Western culture foster a habit of blindness. For all the bustle, a dreary sameness comes to mark the places where we live. We forget that there is a vast depth beneath the apparent surfaces of things.

The eye of aesthetic spirituality sees more than other eyes. Art in general, and photography in particular, helps to facilitate this awakening by granting us epiphanies through its transfigurations of the ordinary. We come to know more than what appears within our line of vision.

As we begin to look at cultivating our capacity for spiritual sight through the medium of photography, there are insights and principles we need to first explore, even before we bring the camera to the eye and open the lens to the world, revealing what is beneath the surface. Beauty is one dimension to explore.

On Beauty

Some, like Augustine, have used the word "beauty" as a name for God, a name that expresses something about the divine nature. Beauty has long been considered one of the great means through which God is revealed to us. To experience beauty is to have your life enlarged—an aesthetic spirituality is about seeing the beauty of God in more and more places. We might begin to see all of life as what the Celts called a "thin place," where heaven and earth are close together.

When our eyes are graced with wonder, the world reveals its wonders to us. What we see is determined by how we see, and each of us is responsible for how we see. For poet John O'Donohue, seeing is not merely a physical act: "The heart of vision is shaped by the state of the soul. When the soul is alive to beauty, we begin to see life in a fresh and vital way." Contemplative practice is one way of taking responsibility for "the how" of our vision. And photography is one path that can help us to cultivate this capacity.

There is a scene in the film *American Beauty* that demonstrates this kind of graced sight. A white plastic bag is caught in the wind, in front of metal doors covered with graffiti. The bag dances in different directions, up and down, side to side, lifted and lowered by the air. Through the lens, the audience is invited to a slow, deliberate seeing, and what begins as a piece of litter on a dirty street becomes a symbol of how, even in the toughest and least expected places, beauty happens. Ricky Fitts, the character showing this image to his friend, murmurs, "Sometimes, there's so much beauty in the world, I can't take it—like my heart's going to cave in."

For brief moments, something transfigures the world around us, as it reveals beauty's radiance. These moments wake us up and train our perceptions. The purpose of art is not to send us to an alternative world but rather to return us, even as our vision has been renewed, to the realm of the ordinary. We don't have to go out and try to take "beautiful" photos. We simply need to pay attention and foster a different kind of seeing.

Jesuit theologian Hans Urs von Balthasar believed that the word "glory" in the Bible indicated the beauty of God. Of truth, goodness, and beauty, the three transcendental attributes of God, it was beauty that, for von Balthasar, was the least obscured by our fallen nature and therefore provides the clearest path to the Beatific Vision. Human encounter with the divine begins in a moment of aesthetic perception, in that glimpse of radiance, mystery, and meaning that we can see in a work of art or in the natural world. In the gospel story of the Transfiguration, beauty becomes a window onto the divine. The burning light that once appeared to Moses in the bush now radiates from Jesus himself: "His face shone like the sun" (Matthew 17:2). For Gregory Palamas, it was the disciples who changed at the Transfiguration, not Christ. Christ was transfigured "not by the addition of something he was not, but by the manifestation to his disciples of what he really was. He opened their eyes so that instead of being blind they could see." Because their perception grew sharper, they were able to behold Christ as he truly is. This journey into photography as a contemplative practice is a journey toward transfigured seeing, toward seeing the world as it really is. By bringing the camera to the eye and allowing an encounter with the holy to open our hearts, we have the possibility for a transformative potential from the photographic encounter. Look through the lens and imagine that it is a portal to a new way of seeing. Let the focus of the frame bring your gaze to the quality of light in this moment or the vibrancy of colors. Like in the film *American Beauty*, let yourself be willing to see the world differently, so that what others see as garbage becomes transfigured through your openness and intention. This isn't always easy, and ultimately it is God's work in us; we just create the right conditions to receive the gift.

Painter Georgia O'Keeffe wrote, "Nobody sees a flower really; it is so small. We haven't time, and to see takes time—like to have a friend takes time." We will only "really see" a flower if we train ourselves to do so, and this training takes time and practice. To peer into a deeper reality is a metaphysical endeavor, requiring that we "see" with more than merely our eyes and that we sense with more than merely our natural senses.

The Art of Beholding

Open my eyes, so that I may behold
wondrous things out of your law.

—Psalm 119:18

God's presence is always before us. The invitation is to shift our vision from seeing the obvious and expected with our physical eyes to beholding the sacred within any given moment with the eyes of our hearts. The word "behold" appears throughout scripture as a way of calling our attention to something important, inviting us to see differently, to observe with care.

Are you familiar with those visual images that on the surface just look like black and white wavy lines? When you sit with it for a while and let your vision relax, suddenly a three-dimensional image emerges. What seemed to be a meaningless pattern actually reveals something beneath the surface. Your visual perception has shifted, and with that shift you can suddenly see differently than before. You are now able to enter a world that was previously invisible to you but was present the whole time.

The art of beholding is like this. "Behold" means to hold something in your gaze. To behold is not to stare or glance; it is not a quick scan or an expectant look. Beholding has a slow and spacious quality to it. Your vision becomes softer as you make room to take in the whole of what you are seeing. There is a reflective and reverential quality to this kind of seeing. You release your expectations of what you think you will see and instead receive what is actually there, while in the process everything can shift. Frederick Franck, in his book *Zen and Art of Seeing*, writes about the patterns we anticipate: "By these labels we recognize everything, and no longer see anything. We know the labels on the bottles, but never taste the wine."

When you cultivate the art of beholding, you nurture your capacity to see the world with the eyes of the heart. Hold your camera in your hand and open yourself to grace and revelation hidden in each moment, just beneath the surface of what seems to be another ordinary moment. Remember, we aren't so concerned here with the technical aspects of photography. Your camera isn't just a tool but a portal.

We are so used to using our capacity for vision to take in our surroundings quickly, to scan over things, to look over or observe, and to confirm what it is we are already thinking. Seeing in this other way takes time and patience. We can't force the hidden dimension of the world to come forth; we can only create a receptive space in our hearts in which it can arrive. In our photography practice, this needs to be cultivated again and again.

Carmelite William McNamara described contemplation as a "long loving look at the real." It is long because it takes time and slowness to see the holy, shimmering presence beneath the surface of things. It is loving because the contemplative act is one that arises from a place of compassion. It is a look at the real, at the truth of things as they are, and not how we want them to be. This means that sometimes when we behold, we see suffering, and we have to stay awake to that experience.

Contemplative seeing and beholding are conscious acts of becoming receptive and dropping as much as possible, our own ego desires and projections. It is only from this space of openness and wonder that we truly see the movement of God in the world.

The Heart as the Source of Vision

You've got to get out of your head and into your heart. Right now your thoughts are in your head, and God seems to be outside you. Your prayer and all your spiritual exercises also remain exterior. As long as you are in your head, you will never master your thoughts, which continue to whirl around your head like snow in a winter's storm or like mosquitoes in the summer's heat.

If you descend into your heart, you will have no more difficulty. Your mind will empty out and your thoughts will dissipate. Thoughts are always in your mind chasing one another about, and you will never manage to get them under control. But if you enter into your heart and can remain there, then every time your thoughts invade, you will only have to descend into your heart and your thoughts will vanish into thin air. This will be your safe haven. Don't be lazy! Descend! You will find life in your heart. There you must live.

—St. Theophan the Recluse[2]

In the innermost depths of my heart I transcend the bounds of my created personhood and discover within myself the direct unmediated presence of the living God. Entry into the deep heart means that I experience myself as God-sourced, God-enfolded, God-transfigured.

—Kallistos Ware[3]

In the writings of scripture and the Christian mystics, the heart is considered to be the primary organ of our physical, emotional, and spiritual well-being. Across religious traditions, it is considered to be the dwelling place of God or Spirit. The heart is at not only the center of our being but also the center of Transcendent realities with which we come into communion through the heart. It is the organ of divine revelation and sense perception, the place from which the spiritual senses operate. St. Benedict begins his Rule inviting us to "listen with the ear of our heart."

The heart is an axial point, a center of unity within the person as a whole. It is an ancient metaphor for the seat of our whole being—to be whole-hearted means to bring our entire selves before God, our intellect, our emotional life, our dreams and intuitions, and our deepest longings. The heart is "at one and the same time a physical reality—the bodily organ located in our chest—and also a psychic and spiritual symbol. Above all it signifies integration and relationship: the integration and unification of the total person within itself, and at the same time the centering and focusing of the total person upon God."[4]

The heart is not just active but also receptive. The heart is the place of meaning-making, where we discover how we are called to be in the world. It is the ground of our being and a symbol of the wholeness of who we are. When we engage photography as a contemplative practice, we are creating art from a heart-centered place. The "eyes of the heart" are eyes that see differently than when we approach things from the mind. Just like the camera, the heart has the capacity for turning its lens toward what it longs to see and then choosing its focus.

Cynthia Bourgeault, in her book *The Wisdom Way of Knowing: Reclaiming an Ancient Tradition to Awaken the Heart*, writes that the instrument we are given to engage most fully in life is our heart: "Not our mind alone, certainly, nor simply the undisciplined riot of our subconscious, but something that both unifies and transcends them from a place of deeper wholeness. Spiritually understood, the heart is an organ of astonishing perceptivity and versatility that when fully awakened and tuned allows us to play our part in the dynamism of creation." The heart, she goes on to say, is not the opposite of the head, nor primarily the emotional receptor. "Rather it is a sensitive, multispectrum instrument of awareness: a huge realm of mind that includes both mental and affective operations (that is, the ability both to think and to feel) and both conscious and subconscious dimensions."[5] The heart is able to perceive the deeper order and coherence of things that on the surface seem random or chaotic. It is through the heart that we can see beyond, beneath, and through. In working with the camera, we can access the heart as this "multispectrum instrument of awareness" and allow our photos to become a conduit for this kind of vision.

"Taking" photos with the head is often an act of analysis or grasping, as when we try to either capture an image or make one that is aesthetically pleasing. "Receiving" photos with the heart is an experience of grace and revelation, an encounter with the sacred.

Miksang and Buddhist Perspectives

Related to Bourgeault's exploration of the heart as the organ of spiritual vision that welcomes in the fullness of possibilities before us—and not just what we expect to see—there is a Buddhist practice of contemplative photography, currently taught under the name of *Miksang*, which is a Tibetan word that translates as "good eye." This Buddhist practice of cultivating contemplative vision developed from the teachings of the Tibetan Buddhist meditation master Chogyam Trungpa Rinpoche. The goal of Miksang is simply to experience the world before distinctions like "beautiful" or "ugly," and "worthy" or "unworthy," get in the way—to see and appreciate the nature of things as they are and express it without interpretation.

This Buddhist form of practice is not meant to be a form of self-expression; in fact, a letting go of "self" is actively cultivated. Miksang seeks to develop a calm and centered state of being in the midst of receiving images, leading to a posture of openness.

In both Christian and Buddhist forms of contemplative photography, the focus is on practicing this way of seeing and being with the camera, letting it spill over into the whole of your life and shift your perspective, so that slowly you are able to see beneath the surface of all life and discover the shimmering presence of truth in all moments. In the contemplative life we begin to explore paradoxes at the heart of things, where we learn to see beneath the labels we apply to everything, so that we don't look actively for "beauty" but allow all things—even those that repel us or bore us—to have room in our vision and consciousness. The paradox is that in the Christian practice, when we free ourselves in this way, we discover a new way of understanding beauty through the camera. We may find that beauty is truly shimmering everywhere, moving our hearts even in the midst of decay or destruction. This is the power of the lens—to help us make space in our field of vision for things regardless of their perceived aesthetic value, so we might discover a deeper landscape, full of unexpected beauty.

The Third Eye

Theologian and Franciscan priest Richard Rohr writes about three kinds of vision in his book *The Naked Now: Learning to See as the Mystics See*. The first kind is our physical vision on the level of seeing the world with our senses. The second kind is a vision that comes with knowledge, as we begin to explain other aspects of the world through learning about them. This vision brings together imagination, intuition, and reason. The third kind of vision Rohr describes as tasting, where we remain in "awe before an underlying mystery, coherence, and spaciousness" that connects us with everything else.[6] The third eye is unitive rather than dualistic. It brings together what seems in opposition on the surface of things.

Rohr goes on to say that the first eye seeing is important; the senses matter. The second eye seeing is also important, but knowledge is not to be confused with depth, or having correct information with the transformation of consciousness itself. The third eye seeing builds on these first two but ventures deeper. "It happens whenever, by some wondrous 'coincidence,' our heart space, our mind space, and our body awareness are all simultaneously open and nonresistant. I like to call it *presence*. It is experienced as a moment of deep inner connection, and it always pulls you, intensely satisfied, into the naked and undefended now, which can involve both profound joy and profound sadness. At that point, you either want to write poetry, pray, or be utterly silent."[7]

From the perspective of photography, our first kind of vision is what we see through the lens. The second kind of vision involves all of the thoughts and judgments we make as we compose an image: about what the image means, about whether it is "good," and so forth. The third kind of vision moves us beyond these, so that the camera draws us into an experience of presence with this moment now, and it becomes a prayer. The practice of contemplative photography invites us into a receptive space where we bring our physical capacity for sight, and we bring our thinking mind, and yet we also allow this third kind of vision to have primacy. Third eye vision, beholding, and seeing with the eyes of the heart or the spiritual senses are all ways of describing this practice. The heart sees new patterns underlying the world and can help bring them into form. The camera as a spiritual tool helps us to tend to the coherence and presence beneath the surface of things.

Of course, even photography itself and our preoccupation with "capturing" images can become a barrier to this deeper vision. Susan Sontag, in *On Photography*, writes, "A way of certifying experience, taking photographs is also a way of refusing it—by limiting experience to a search for the photogenic, by converting experiences into an image, a souvenir."[8] Depending on how we approach our photographic encounters, it can also become a substitute for really seeing and participating in life. This is the difference between photography as a way of recording life or for fine arts and as a contemplative practice, opening us onto a wider and deeper field of vision.

The person who sees participates in life; the person who merely looks does not.

If at any time in working with this book you find yourself grasping for your camera, wanting to "capture the moment," consider pausing and letting it go by and letting yourself instead receive the shimmering presence or image with your heart.

Thomas Merton as Photographer

We can trace some of the roots of photography—an undeniably modern art form—as a Christian contemplative practice to the most famous modern monk, Thomas Merton. In 1968, Merton wrote to a friend soon after he had received the gift of a camera: "What a joy of a thing to work with . . . the camera is the most eager and helpful of all beings, all full of happy suggestions: "Try this! Do it that way!" Reminding me of things I have overlooked and cooperating in the creation of new worlds. So Simply. This is a Zen camera."[9]

At this point in time Merton had been making photos for several years already, but now his photography took on more impetus. He discovered the lens of the camera to be a valuable tool for contemplative practice. Merton brought his camera on walks and photographed what moved him, letting the camera reveal what was there rather than bringing to the camera what he expected to see. Merton discovered in photography an alignment with his exploration of Zen practice.

Merton had begun his first serious exploration of photography in January 1962 when he visited a Shaker village near his monastery: "Marvelous, silent, vast spaces around the old buildings. Cold, pure light, and some grand trees. So cold my finger could no longer feel the shutter release. Some marvelous subjects. How the blank side of a frame house can be so completely beautiful I cannot imagine. A completely miraculous achievement of forms."[10] As he developed friendships with other artists and photographers, he wrote to them about his discoveries.

One of Merton's most well-known photographs is titled "The Sky Hook." He wrote that the picture "is the only known photograph of God." The composition of the photo is balanced between positive and negative space, a steel hook cuts through the top center of the image, curled toward the sky. The hook is empty, holding nothing. It is an evocative image that acts somewhat like a Zen koan by inviting us to see beyond preconceived and neatly packaged ideas.

MEDITATION:
THE PRACTICE OF BEHOLDING

Beholding a person or place is a conscious and receptive act of releasing our inner judgments and projections as much as possible. From this place of openness, we are then free to experience the grace and movement of God.

Choose a familiar place where for just ten minutes you can engage in the spiritual practice of beholding—a place such as a favorite café or park, where there is some human activity.

Take a deep breath. Then intentionally shift your focus from ordinary seeing and noticing, to an experience of beholding which infuses the moment with a sense of reverence. See if you can notice a physical, emotional, and spiritual shift in opening yourself to simply being with whatever and whomever arrives in your line of vision. Offer them abundant compassion and love. Notice what this stirs in your own heart.

PHOTOGRAPHIC EXPLORATION:
FIFTY IMAGES AND ONE IMAGE

Sit in a relaxed and comfortable position and find a point on which to focus in front of you. It could be anything that isn't moving—a chair, a vase, or a point on the wall or floor. Take a few moments to let yourself focus completely on this point without hardening into a stare.

Then slowly become aware of your peripheral vision, while maintaining this point of focus. See if you can keep your focus while also making room in your sight for the field surrounding this point in a soft and relaxed way. This is the kind of vision we will cultivate in our photography practice—holding the tension between focus and

diffuse awareness, keeping the gaze soft, receiving what is around you rather than trying to penetrate into its meaning. Bring this soft awareness to the world as you walk and receive images.

Choose an object from your everyday life. It could be anything that you engage with daily but that often falls under your radar of real attention. Allow yourself fifteen minutes with your camera, begin with a soft gaze, and then become curious about this object and see if you can make fifty images of it. Become intimate with it, look at it from different angles, and place it in different kinds of light, or against different background colors. See what new things you can discover in this process. Try not to force this experience. Keep a connection to your heart while working with the camera. Then, for the next five days, take *one* photo per day only. As you move through the day notice what really shimmers forth, what really captures your attention. Then, after that single photo, put your camera away for the day. If another great image comes forth, be with it without the camera. Savor its qualities. See what you notice in yourself by having to limit your photography in this way. Is it freeing? Frustrating? If you find yourself frustrated, return to your heart. Let go of the need to analyze this experience. Sometimes just a single image is enough, when we bring ourselves fully present to it.

REFLECTION QUESTIONS

- What is it like to shift your focus from looking to seeing?
- Which of your own physical senses seems most keenly attuned to the world?
- Which sense do you savor most? Visual images, music, food, aroma, or touch? What does this reveal to you about the way you perceive the sacred in the world?

2

PRACTICES AND
TOOLS TO CULTIVATE VISION

The eye, when it opens, is like the dawn breaking in the night. When it opens a new world is there. The eye is also the mother of distance. When the eye opens, it shows that the world and others are outside us, distant from us. . . . Love is the light in which we see each thing in its true origin, nature and destiny. If we could look at the world in a loving way, then the world would rise up before us full of invitation, possibility and depth.

—John O'Donohue

And now here is my secret, a very simple secret:
It is only with the heart that one can see clearly;
What is essential is invisible to the eye.

—Antoine de Saint-Exupery

"Receiving" Rather than "Taking" Photos

Contemplative practice is a receptive practice. We make ourselves available for grace to break in; we open ourselves to listen and ponder. In visio divina, we move our awareness into our hearts and let our vision arise from this place of integration rather than analysis, and receptivity rather than grasping after the things we desire. Our intention is to see things from a new perspective, but the paradox is that this longing requires us to relinquish our usual ways of relating to the world.

We often use the word "take" to describe our relationship with photography. Our culture emphasizes taking time, taking what's mine, and taking a break. What we are endeavoring to do in this process, however, is to *receive* (rather than *take*) the gifts around us, to be present enough so that, when the photographic moment arrives, we are able to receive it fully, with our whole hearts.

"Taking photos" is a common phrase, and changing that perception and process (especially if you use a smartphone, Lomo, or other disposable camera) may be hard to break, but I gently invite you to consider what reframing this process might be like for you and what it evokes in you. I invite you to bring a new awareness to how words and phrases can shape our experience and practices.

Rather than "taking" photos or "shooting" them or even "making" photos, we will practice "receiving" images as gift. The traditional words for photography are possessive and aggressive. Yet the actual mechanism of photography is that light is reflected off of a subject and *received* by the camera through the lens opening. We can create conditions for a "good" photo, but ultimately we must stand in a posture of receiving and see what actually shows up in the image.

The poet Rainer Maria Rilke writes in one of his poems of "no forcing or holding back." When we are receptive we let go of our agendas and expectations. We allow ourselves to see beneath preconceived ideas. Rather than going after what we want in life, or "forcing," we cultivate a contentment with what actually is. Similarly, instead of "holding back" and merely observing life or falling asleep to it, we stay awake and alert, participating fully in its messiness and we keep our eyes open for the holy presence in its midst.

Photographing in this way can become an act of revelation. One of the gifts of art in general, and photography in particular, is that the artist can offer others this vision of the graced ordinary moment.

This brings to mind the monastic value of hospitality. In chapter 53 of his Rule, Benedict writes, "Let all guests who arrived be received like Christ." When the stranger arrives—that which is unexpected, strange, and mysterious—we are called to recognize the holy presence shimmering there. This means inviting strangers into our world without imposing our own agenda on them. In contemplative practice and photography, it means staying open and curious to what we might discover when we don't know what to expect, when we make the effort to see beneath the surfaces. It means gazing on scenes before us that feel strange and making space to receive them fully.

Being with Inner Voices

When I lead in-person retreats and classes, I always pause a moment near the beginning to encourage participants to check in with themselves regularly during the next few weeks of journeying with the material. Since I can't look you in the eye and say this, imagine me gazing on you with love as I utter these words.

One of the most important things I think I can teach is learning to make space to listen to your own deepest longings and begin to trust those more. There are all kinds of reasons we learn to doubt ourselves. Part of growth is taking risks, which I encourage, but I equally encourage gentleness with yourself. When we begin a journey like this, which for each of you is an extension of the journey you've already begun, we open ourselves to our vulnerability, to the tender dreams just beginning to bud within us, and to the risk inherent in expressing our deepest selves.

Remember what I have said about the field of expressive arts as primarily focused on healing and self-expression, on process instead of product. Through this lens the arts become a place of discovery. So when I make suggestions for the meditations, photographic explorations, and the reflection questions, I encourage you to enter into the experience as a prayer, a communion with your Creative Source, and see if you can release your worries about making a beautiful product. As an authentic expression of your longings and unique soul, it will inevitably have its own beauty. There is certainly a place for the role of craft and fine art in photography. But our focus here in this book is on allowing your authentic expression as a response to being fully present to come through as much as possible. We are cultivating our ability to see.

When internal judgments arise in the process of making photos—and as human beings, they most certainly will—simply notice them with curiosity and compassion, and contemplate where else in your life those voices arise. *Allow photography and the process of receiving and gazing upon your photos to become a container for your internal awareness.* The same is true for writing; allow yourself to express whatever is true for you in the process, and notice where the blocks, judgments, and voices arise, gently and with compassion for yourself. *Give yourself permission to make mistakes, to make "bad art,"* or to write something that doesn't sound close to perfect. Remember this is about the process of discovery and not about creating beautiful products.

Lectio Divina and Visio Divina

In its original form, lectio divina is an ancient practice of being present to a sacred text in a heart-centered way. We are often taught in churches to think through our prayers—reciting words and formulas that are valuable elements of our shared traditions but only one window into God's presence. In the prayer form of lectio divina, we invite God to speak to us unmediated. Our memories, images, and feelings become an important context for experiencing God's voice active in us, and we discover it when we pray in a heart-centered way. The words that move through us break open God's invitation to us in this moment of our lives and call us to respond in some way. In lectio we are invited to surrender into the prayer. The thinking mind will try to control what unfolds, or analyze and judge the process.

When we pray lectio we see the words of scripture as God's living words being spoken to our hearts in this moment. The prayer is an encounter with a God who is active and intimate with our lives. The primary action of this prayer is listening for how God is already praying within us.

The invitation of lectio divina is to cultivate a heart-centered intimacy with the sacred texts, which is a different way of being with them than pure interpretive reasoning. Listening, savoring, and responding are different qualities of being that are cultivated in this practice. The purpose of this practice is that we gradually bring these qualities of being to the whole of our lives, and everything becomes a potential sacred text through which God can speak to us.

St. Benedict in his Rule required every monk to spend significant time each day in lectio divina as a contemplative way of being with scripture. When we pray lectio, we are invited to move our awareness away from a purely rational and analytical response to the text and instead to bring the whole of ourselves through a heart-centered awareness—including the intuitive, emotional, and experiential sides—to the experience.

Lectio involves a series of inner movements that are more spiral than linear. We begin our practice by moving from step to step, allowing the progression to become a part of ourselves so that gradually the rhythm takes root and we can let it unfold in its own way.

The four primary movements of lectio divina are as follows:

> Read (*lectio*): Read and listen for a word or phrase that calls
> to us in this moment.
> Reflect (*meditatio*): Savor the word, and allow it to unfold
> within you.
> Respond (*oratio*): Listen for the invitation.
> Rest (*contemplatio*): Rest in stillness.

Like other meditation practices, our time in lectio divina can become a container for awareness of inner movements and voices—what stirs in us during this time is a microcosm of our daily lives. As you pray lectio, notice any distractions and gently release them. When this happens, let go of self-judgment and return to the practice.

For the purposes of this book and our focus on photography as a contemplative practice, we will adapt the four steps of lectio divina slightly to pray in a visual way, through what we might call "visio divina," or sacred seeing, with the world and with our photos. Seeing with the "eyes of our heart" means to see from the wholeness we already are. We gaze to receive what is true in the world. In the meditation section of this chapter is an outline and invitation into this prayer practice.

Contemplative Walking

We have never seen anything like this.

—Mark 2:1–12

Another one of the foundational exercises or practices in this book is making a commitment to going out in the world with your camera in hand and cultivating a stance of slow attentiveness and receptivity.

One of the ways that I make space to receive things fully, which has become my daily spiritual practice, is by going for a contemplative walk each morning. This walk combines many different elements that have developed over the years in my prayer, but its primary purpose is to cultivate in me a contemplative presence to the world and to listen to what God has to say to me: receiving, rather than making or taking. It is also a way of honoring the seasons of the earth and of my soul. With each walk I listen for the invitation of nature to my heart. Often my camera is with me as a tool to grow in my presence; it helps me to learn how to slow down enough to really *see* things.

Contemplative walking doesn't necessarily mean walking slowly, although there is a deliberateness to its pace. Make time to go for a long walk, and as you walk, see if you can allow yourself to not have to "get" anywhere. As you take each step, listen closely to your own intuition about where you are being moved to go next. Slow down enough to see what is around you, notice the details of things—the many shades of flowers, the texture of tree bark, architectural details on houses, and even the patterns on manhole covers or gutters. You aren't looking for something beautiful; you are trying to be present to life as it is and respond to the call of the world to your heart, and in this process you will discover beauty. You will begin to see the world with new eyes.

Your photographic journey is essentially a mini-pilgrimage. Sometimes we think we have to journey to faraway places to have a transformative experience. Monastic wisdom tells us the sacred is right here, right now, and if we can't see it right before us, traveling around the world won't change things.

MEDITATION:
LEARNING THE ART OF VISIO DIVINA

Sometime in the days following your experience of a contemplative walk and photographic explorations, I invite you to engage in a process of visio divina with one or more of your images. You are going to pray with one of your photos. Choose one that shimmers for you or stirs an energetic response. You don't have to know why; trust your intuitive sense, and notice which image is calling for more time to dwell with it. You can print it out or display it on your computer monitor, and it will be the sacred text for your time of prayer.

Visio divina means sacred seeing and is essentially an application of the rhythms of lectio to a prayer of "gazing." Gazing is looking upon something with the eyes of the heart. It is not a hard or penetrating stare but a soft receptive way of being with an image.

Take a few moments to move inward, closing your eyes. Become aware of your body, and shift in any way you need to right now. Slowly become aware of your breath, being present to the rhythm of inhale and exhale. As you breathe in, call to mind the image of the Spirit of God breathing life into you. As you breathe out, allow your body to relax and release into this moment of time. Let your exhale bring you to a deeper surrender and experience of presence. Take just a few moments to be present to this life-sustaining rhythm.

Gently begin to allow your breath to move your awareness from your head, your thinking and analyzing center, down into your heart center, that place of receptivity, intuition, and experience. Place your hand on your heart for just a moment to experience a physical connection. Take a moment to notice what you are feeling right now, making room for it without trying to change anything. Simply be present to whatever is true for you right now. Remember that the mystics tell us that God dwells in the sacred centers of our hearts, and bring some holy compassion to whatever your experience is right now.

From this heart-centered place, slowly open your eyes and cast a gentle gaze upon your photo with the eyes of your heart. Take a few moments to allow your eyes to wander over the whole landscape of the image, exploring all of its shapes, colors, contours, details, and symbols. Allow yourself to simply be present to the details of this image.

Gradually notice if there is a place on the photo where your eye is being invited to rest. Try not to think this through too much. Notice both experiences of resonance and dissonance, where your energy is being drawn or where it is being resisted.

What is the place on the image calling to you—is it a symbol, color, or expression? Take a few moments to simply be present to this in a gentle way.

Begin to allow this place on the photo to unfold in your imagination. You might want to close your eyes again and notice what memories, images, and feelings are being stirred within you. Allow space within yourself for these to emerge, simply noticing your experience and being present to what is stirring. Rest here for a few moments without judgment.

Slowly begin to notice if an invitation begins to emerge from these memories, feelings, and images moving in you. In the concrete circumstances of your life right now, what awareness or action is God calling you to? What is my invitation in this moment of my life? How am I being called to respond?

Take another few moments to be present to however this invitation wants to be expressed.

Connect to your breath once more. Breathe in gratitude for whatever has been revealed. Breathe out and release the images moving within you and rest for a few moments in gratitude, simply relishing the experience of stillness and being in the presence of God.

In these final moments of prayer, allow your breath to slowly and gently bring your awareness back to the room. As you open your eyes, take just another moment to gaze upon the photo and take it in as a whole. See if there is anything else you notice right now, and then bring your meditation to a close. I invite you to take a few moments now to write any reflections in your journal and transition gently back to your day.

As you become more comfortable with praying in this way, and allowing visual elements to be a "text" for prayer, you can begin to bring this spirit of visio divina with you even as you are out walking and photographing the world around you, and not just in reflecting on those images. As you receive your images, pay attention to moments that seem to shimmer and make space within your heart to be with whatever feelings or memories these stir, trusting that God is at work in the process. Over time, you might discover that there is an invitation being offered to you in this time of slowing down and deepening your way of seeing the world.

Photographic Exploration: Receiving Images

Go on a contemplative walk that will also be a photographic journey. Bring your camera with you, and imagine you are heading out on a pilgrimage that is a journey of discovery. The symbols and images you discover can become catalysts for deeper self-exploration. Begin the walk with a brief time to center yourself, and become aware of the sacred presence dwelling within you. Move your awareness

to your heart center. Ask for guidance and wisdom to see everyday things with the eyes of the heart. Bring a soft gaze to the world. As you walk, be present to what is calling for your attention. Then go for a walk in your neighborhood, down familiar streets, but walk slowly and see what you notice. Let your camera be a window onto a new way of seeing. Receive the images that come.

REFLECTION QUESTIONS

The moment one gives close attention to anything, even a blade of grass, it becomes a mysterious, awesome, indescribably magnificent world in itself.

—Henry Miller[1]

- Notice your own places of resistance. Have you made time to be outside with your camera receiving the gifts that find you? What might need to shift to create more room for this experience?

- The photographer Dorothea Lange wrote, "The camera is an instrument which teaches people to see without a camera."[2] Are you noticing anything about how you see the world when you are not on your photographic journey? Are there moments when you receive a gift and rush to grab your cameras and completely miss what was happening? Photography is simply a tool to cultivate our ability to be present to the world.

- As you prepare to begin this journey of seeing with the eyes of the heart, what are the things, habits, beliefs, messages, and other blocks that keep you from being fully free? What do you need to lay aside for this journey of deeper vision?

- Have you had a moment yet these last few days of giving close attention to something and discovering a "mysterious, awesome, indescribably magnificent world"?

3

The Dance of Light and Shadow

Once I can recognize the divine image where I don't want to see the divine image, then I have learned how to see. It's really that simple. And here's the rub: I'm not the one that is doing the seeing. It's like there is another pair of eyes inside of me seeing through me, seeing with me, seeing in me. God can see God everywhere, and God in me can see God everywhere.

—**Richard Rohr**

The soul that is united with God sees the world with God's eyes. That soul, like God, sees what otherwise is rendered invisible and irrelevant.

—**Dorothee Soelle**

Contemplating Light

Light is the medium of photography. The word "photography" was invented in 1839 by Sir John Herschel and is derived from the Greek words *photos* meaning "light" and *graphé* meaning "representation by means of lines" or "drawing with light."

Your digital camera's electronic sensor, much like the film that preceded it, makes a record of light. The sensor converts each light strike as a change in electrical charge, and this is what is stored as an image. This is also similar to how your eyes work; photons strike the retina's rod and cone cells and they respond to the light.

We see sunlight as having hue, chroma (the colorfulness in relation to another color), saturation (intensity), lightness (value or tone), and brightness (reflectiveness). Consider the quality of light on a sunny, cloudless, early summer morning and then the same sunny cloudless day at noon or late afternoon. Then there are the midwinter days that are so grey all day long it always feels like evening. What do you notice and appreciate about the hue of light at different seasons? I love the golden light of an autumn evening and the way the angle of the sun illuminates the jewel tones of a thousand leaves.

Whether you are conscious of it or not, we each have an incredible range of experiences of the quality of light at different moments. And one of the gifts of photography is cultivating our appreciation for the hundreds of varying qualities of light.

Light is an oft-used metaphor for God or divine activity in scripture. In Genesis, God says, "Let there be light" and light appears. "I am the light of the world," Jesus said; "Whoever follows me will never walk in darkness, but will have the light of life" (John 8:12).

Sometimes the tension between light and darkness becomes problematic in scripture, when the dark is symbolic of blindness or ignorance. In other places, however, we read of "treasures of darkness" (Isaiah 45:3) and the proclamation of the psalmist: "Darkness is not dark for you, and night shines as the day. Darkness and light are but one" (Psalm 139:12).

In photography, both light and shadow are required to make an image, and so the medium invites us to consider ways to integrate both of these gifts in our own lives and contemplations.

Opaqueness to Transparency

Thomas Merton described the contemplative life as a journey from opaqueness to transparency, from the place where things are dark, thick, impenetrable, and closed to the place where these same things are translucent, open, and offer a vision far beyond themselves.[1]

In the art of photography, we might imagine the difference between having a lens that is open and clean of debris, and one that has become smudged with dust, obscuring the possibility of seeing clearly. Our own capacity to perceive this God-given reality of transparency and interconnectedness has been diminished and distorted. It has in fact become "hidden." Merton used such phrases as "hidden wholeness" and "hidden ground of love" to name this unperceived but, nevertheless, foundational reality. This reality is hidden by our inability to see it. This inability arises from the incrustation and overlay of cultural values and distortions that give rise to the development of false selves with limited consciousness.

How do we move to perceive that transparency? We change our perception—inner work is the key. "The first step in the interior life . . . is unlearning our wrong ways of seeing, tasting, feeling, and so forth, and [acquiring] a few of the right ones. The 'right' way of seeing involves in part 'the ability to respond to reality, to see the value and beauty of ordinary things.'"[2]

When we approach photography as a contemplative practice, we engage consciously in this movement from opaqueness to transparency, from shadow to illuminated clarity. We move from the idea of images "taken" from the world as a property to be possessed to images received from the world as a gift of abundance and invitation. We move from looking at the world to see what we can gain to gazing on the world to see what gifts we might receive. These are all essential aspects of the contemplative path and are cultivated by our shift in vision.

Contemplative practice has the capacity to help us relate to time differently. Rather than experiencing time as a string of unconnected events or accidents, when we open our hearts to receive a deeper vision, we discover an inner coherence to the world and a grounding presence holding everything together. When we hold the camera in this open-hearted way, we encounter moments when time opens out onto eternity and we lose track of the minutes ticking away. We are lifted beyond ourselves into the realm of the holy, which pulses before us each moment. Light reveals connections everywhere. One of the great gifts of art-making is an experience of "forgetting" ourselves and our self-consciousness, and stepping into something much bigger. Photography can connect us to time outside of time. Suddenly, we realize we have been completely absorbed in our art and prayer and feel transported to an altogether different kind of experience.

The desert father Evagrius Ponticus called contemplation *theoria physike*, which means a vision (*theoria*) into the nature of things (*physike*). To attain this vision, Evagrius said spiritual discipline is necessary. He describes the discipline of *pratike*, which is the peeling away of the blindfolds that prevent us from seeing clearly. The photographer-contemplative, then, is someone who is able to see things as they really are, and is able to be present to beauty and suffering with compassion because we have been able to extend this compassionate gaze to ourselves.

Shadow Work

> You must have shadow and light source both.
>
> **—Rumi**[3]

As contemplatives, we are invited to peel away the blindfolds that prevent us from seeing ourselves clearly as well. In psychological terms, the aspect of ourselves that is opaque or hidden from our awareness is called the shadow. The shadow contains all of the elements we disown, both the "negative" aspects of ourselves as well as the "positive." We discover these aspects by paying attention to our projections. Those people in our lives to whom we respond with a strong energetic charge, whether strongly disliking or strongly liking, generally carry a disowned part of ourselves within them.

Photography is a medium that engages both light and shadow to create art. Light without the shadowed elements creates an overexposed image without any texture or depth. Shadow without light leaves only an underexposed image without any recognizable form. This chapter invites you to pay attention to the play and dance of light and shadow in the images you receive as a way of tending to your own invitations to explore the light and shadow within yourself. Through this process we slowly begin to see ourselves as we really are and embrace our own wholeness.

Psychotherapist and author David Richo writes in his book *Shadow Dance*,

> Our dark shadow can be called the cellar of our unexamined shame. Our positive shadow is an attic of our unclaimed valuables. . . . Every person to whom we react with strong fear, desire, repulsion, or admiration is a twin of our own inner unacknowledged life. We have qualities, both positive and negative, that appear visibly in others, but are invisible in us and to us.[4]

What strongly attracts or repels us gives us clues to these hidden parts of ourselves. This is why I encourage people to notice images that create a strong sense of either resonance or dissonance in the creative process. Anything that stirs your energy is valuable for the invitation it is extending to look within for the source. We project those aspects onto others, which is why we experience such a strong reaction to certain people.

The art-making journey in general stirs up inner judgment and resistance, rooted in parts of ourselves we reject or that were rejected by others in the past. Many of us have negative memories of an art teacher or parent who responded unfavorably or unenthusiastically to our creations and squelched our spontaneous expression. The practice of photography invites us to notice these experiences in ourselves and make room for them. Often our immediate response to difficult inner material rising up is to reject it and push it out of our awareness, to think better thoughts. The art of photography reminds us that light and shadow are both essential for each other to create something beautiful and meaningful. They both need to be welcomed in, in equal measure. We can cultivate this both through awareness of our subject matter and through attention to our inner process by noticing the thoughts and judgments that arise for us while creating art.

This is an essential part of the journey Jesus makes in the desert. He encounters the devil, the symbol for the dark shadow of our individual and collective selves. He engages the devil in dialogue—a conversation unfolds, and he is able to subvert the desire for power he is confronted with by naming it and bringing it to light.

The Golden Shadow

Carl Jung called our denied creative potential the "Golden Shadow." While we often talk about the shadow in the psyche (or the dark/confusing/disturbing elements of a photograph) as shameful or frightening aspects of ourselves or in the photograph, a realm we have explored, for Jung there was another kind of shadow: the Golden Shadow is our unclaimed beauty. The Golden Shadow is the key to finding out what our unique strengths are and discovering that they are hidden in our deepest weaknesses. This is the soul part of ourselves that is meant to offer love, healing, and joy to the often dark world we live in. This is also what it means to see with spiritual eyes: to welcome in the wholeness of who we are, dark and light alike. Photography has the capacity to teach us how to see all of ourselves as graced, by slowly teaching us to allow more and more possibilities into the frame.

Making creative expression a priority in our lives is one way of reclaiming the Golden Shadow aspects of ourselves. When we honor our deep calling to give form to what is within us, we bring healing. Engaging in this work with photography is one dimension of this: committing to a regular practice, carrying your camera always with you, and making time to reflect on your discoveries.

Sometimes we choose not to let our light shine because we are afraid of the responsibility that living into our full strength carries. Living into our gifts often creates tension in our relationships, or elicits envy from others. As we allow ourselves the time and resources to do the things we love, like receive images through photography, it may bring up conflicts in our lives.

The Work of Integration

Contemplating your shadow is a tender process. It has remained hidden to us for a reason, perhaps someone shamed us as a child for being too loud or someone judged us for being too expressive. Through the creative process we begin to invite back in all the rejected parts of ourselves. Rather than rejecting darkness as somehow evil, the shadow invites us to integrate it to come to a place of greater wholeness. We would do well to remember again how essential shadow is to the art of photography, in making a meaningful image, rather than one that is washed out by too much light. The shadow is also connected to the monastic principle of hospitality. St. Benedict wrote in his Rule to welcome in the stranger as Christ. This is both an outer act as well as an inner one—the more we grow capable of welcoming in the strangers within our own hearts, the more we grow in our compassion for the strangers we meet in the world.

Theologian Gregory Mayers, in his book on desert spirituality, describes the deep self-trance we enter when ruled by our shadow energy.

> The deep self-trance constricts our vision to preferred patterns of perception, a security matrix that blunts or masks the uncomfortable edge of our anxiety over the unknown. In other words, we see what we *want* to see, what we have been *taught* to see, what we are *told* to see, what we *expect* to see. We *construct* our world, extracting from the scene before us that which we prefer and leaving aside whatever is at odds with our preferences.[5]

This brings us back to photography as a practice of cultivating our capacity to see things as they really are. The spiritual dimension of sight allows us to welcome in all that feels uncomfortable in the world both around us as well as within us. The more we practice this in one realm, the more it impacts the other, as we often judge something outside of ourselves as "ugly" that we reject internally as well. Our commitment to visio divina and seeing the world as a sacred text, and everything as worthy of our attention and presence, rather than divided between what is "ugly" and "beautiful," or as a mere imitation of our own expectations, means that we might begin to see this as true within our own hearts as well.

The path toward seeing things as they really are is through contemplative practice. If you are feeling some resistance to reading this material on shadow work, that is a good sign. Resistance usually means you are touching into something deep and powerful.

We all have places in our lives where we feel divided. This is what happens with our unconscious, shadow material; it leaves us feeling divided against ourselves. The contemplative journey invites us always toward greater freedom. Through the lens of our cameras we discover our ability to be present to the world in new ways. As we practice this, we also learn to be present to ourselves in new ways.

MEDITATION:
DIALOGUE BETWEEN LIGHT AND SHADOW

Notice if you have any resistance to exploring the shadows. Name how you are feeling, and allow it to have space in you. Pay attention to your dreams while working with this material—especially dreams that present disturbing characters to you—and contemplate how these figures might be a part of your unconscious life.

Begin this experience by intentionally entering some quiet inner space, slowing down your breath and your thoughts, and settling into stillness.

Let your breath draw your awareness down to your heart center. Notice whatever feelings you are having right now without trying to change them. Simply breathe into them, making space to have an experience of them in your body, without resisting or holding on to anything.

Notice the quality of your thoughts right now. Is your mind feeling active and chatty? See if you can bring your breath to your mind and create some spaciousness there, simply letting thoughts and expectations go as they arise.

Return your awareness to your heart center and imagine drawing on the infinite well of compassion within you. Then imagine you are crossing a threshold even more deeply inward. From this space, call to your imagination a part of yourself that feels hidden. Perhaps it is a time when you felt lost or alone, or when you experienced a great loss and submerged the feelings underground, a wounded dimension of yourself. It could be any kind of personality trait in others that makes you highly uncomfortable. Any hidden or denied aspect of ourselves is a shadow self. Again, notice what rises up for you and welcome it in, seeing if this part has a name to offer. Perhaps it is something that you have gotten in touch with through your photographs, that feels somehow "unworthy" of your attention. Have there been scenes or subjects that you turn away from with your camera? Do these give you any insight into aspects of yourself you turn away from internally?

Consider writing a dialogue between you and one of your shadow qualities. We have these ongoing conversations all the time internally between conflicting sides of ourselves. Something about articulating this outward can help us to see the inward dialogue so much more clearly (and we spend a lot of energy keeping up those conversations!) This can be a playful process—engaging your hidden inner voices with curiosity and compassion. Write a snippet of conversation between yourself and your shadow, and see what emerges, what wants to be given voice. What images come to mind as you welcome this part in?

Then call upon a "light" aspect of yourself—one that you are fully aware of, that perhaps you live from on a daily basis, and would bring balance or healing to the submerged part. Trust whatever response comes up. This might be a professional identity or role in your family, for example, somewhere you experience a sense of strength. Any identity of which you are aware can be considered to be a light self, an aspect of ourselves that is not hidden. Consider again your practice of photography. What are the images you are drawn to receive through the lens? Are there particular kinds of subjects or themes you are drawn to again and again? How might this be a reflection of a part of yourself that feels strong and beautiful? Notice again any images that arise in connection with this part.

Then, in your imagination, enter into a dialogue between these two parts—the familiar and the unknown, the light and the shadow. Let them have some time to be in dialogue. Let these parts be respectful and welcoming of one another, while also naming what each one needs from you and from each other. You might do this in your imagination or in a journal. Ask each one what its gift is for you and what is its challenge. How might this process let you bring even more awareness to your photography and what you choose to see and what you choose to ignore?

When your conversation has come to a natural close, thank both of these parts, letting go of your focused attention on them. Return to an awareness of your breath, and let your breath gently bring your awareness back to the room.

Allow some time to be with what has emerged in this meditation. You may want to do some writing or drawing of the different images.

PHOTOGRAPHIC EXPLORATION: LIGHT

Explore the infinite possibilities for qualities of light. Receive photos at different times of day, pay attention to indirect and direct light— out in the sunlight or in the shade, and the light that comes from your evening lamps or streetlamps. If the weather changes in the

days ahead, notice how clouds and sun affect the way you perceive the light. Even take note of where you stand in relationship to something and how it changes the light.

Let yourself become obsessed with the quality of light. Notice light rippling across a lake, reflecting off walls, and illuminating the skin of a loved one.

Start right now: Raise your eyes from this book and look around the room for the ways light is moving through the space around you. Is there sunlight coming through the window? Is it evening and you have a lamp on illuminating a small circle? Is there a slant to the light? A hue? Do you notice hints of gold or blue or some other color?

The midday sun is when the sun is highest and brightest. Photography in this light tends to have strong shadows and overexposed areas, and colors become more alive. On a cloudy day, the clouds act like a diffuser, dispersing light and softening shadows, light shifting moment by moment.

The quality of light at dusk can be magical—photographers have called this time of day the "golden hour." Make some photos where light is the focus. See what you discover as you open your eyes.

PHOTOGRAPHIC EXPLORATION: SHADOW

Engage in your contemplative walk. Try going out in the early morning or at dusk when the shadows will be longer. In the late afternoon to evening, notice how the shadows slowly become longer until they finally disappear with the sun below the horizon. The invitation is to practice being as fully present as you can, gazing with eyes of the heart, noticing what you discover in the process.

Be aware of the moments when your focus becomes distracted or rushed, or your mind fills with judgments. Hold these gently in

your awareness with compassion and curiosity. As you walk, continue to notice what is inviting you to pay attention. Receive each invitation as a gift and as a catalyst for your own reflection and inner growth. Notice the different colors and hues of shadows. Play with silhouettes.

Return home and journal about anything you noticed. Take some time to reflect on what you discovered in the process.

If there is no sunlight to cast shadows in your part of the world as you read this chapter, seek out streetlights in the evening or play at home with angling light against a wall and discovering what kinds of shadows you can make. Working with shadows can be a playful process as well.

Photographic Exploration: Wabi-Sabi

Wabi-sabi is a beauty of things imperfect, impermanent,
and incomplete.
It is a beauty of things modest and humble.
It is a beauty of things unconventional.

—**Leonard Koren**[6]

In the Japanese Buddhist tradition is the term *wabi-sabi*, which refers
to the beauty we find in imperfection and things declining or falling
apart. It is a way of honoring that everything is impermanent and we
are always in a state of both becoming and falling away. The seasons
reveal this wisdom to us with the flowering and fullness of spring

and summer, and the release, decay, and rest found in autumn and winter.

Your invitation for this exploration is to take your camera out into the world and intentionally cast your gaze upon things that others would turn away from. Let this be a time of meditation on how you find the sacred presence shimmering here, in places of imperfection and moments of decay. If we take this journey of seeing with the eyes of the heart seriously, we are called to find the sacred in all things, even what seems "ugly" or in a state of decay. This is another aspect of reclaiming shadow elements.

REFLECTION QUESTIONS

- What has the practice of photography been revealing to you about the elements of your dark shadow—that which you reject as unworthy in yourself?

- What has been revealed through your images about the elements of your positive shadow—all of your untapped creative potential?

- When softening your gaze and beholding the world around you in a visual prayer, what do you discover in the interplay between shadow and light?

- What shadows are being illuminated by seeing with eyes of the heart?

- How has your appreciation for the qualities of light grown through your photographic exploration?

4

WHAT IS HIDDEN AND WHAT IS REVEALED?

Lord, purge our eyes to see
Within the seed a tree
Within the glowing egg a bird,
Within the shroud a butterfly.
Till, taught by such we see . . .
Beyond all creatures, Thee.

—Christina Rossetti

We can now think of vision as a deeply reciprocal event, a participatory activity in which both the seer and the seen are dynamic players. To see is to interact with the visible, to act and be acted upon. It is participation in the ongoing evolution of the visible world.

—David Abram

Storytelling and Reframing

In addition to painting our images with shadow and light, the other primary tool of photography is the frame. When you look through the lens of your camera, you are making choices with each image of what to include and what to exclude, what to hide and what to reveal, and what to focus on and what to allow to become diffuse or blurry. This is a process of visual discernment, and when your awareness of this is heightened, you can become more aware of the choices you make and what they invite you to become aware of in your own life.

When you receive a photo, you are receiving a story about a moment in time. The elements within the frame shape that story, create tension, and both reveal and conceal. Each of us lives out a story as well. Sometimes the story we tell about ourselves needs to shift, and we call this shift reframing.

Are there stories you tell about who you are that might need to change? For example, in discovering some of your shadow elements (both light and dark) and dialoguing with them, what is the bigger story of who you are? What have you been excluding from the frame of your vision? What do the eyes of your heart reveal?

Photography can become a practice of shifting the story, to highlight different elements. Perhaps you have always told the story about what a kind and good-hearted person you are. This is a wonderful story to tell, but maybe in your shadow work you discovered a bit of fierceness there, the part of yourself that wants to speak out against the small (and large) injustices of daily life. Or maybe what is being revealed is a longing for a different kind of life that would rock the boat of the life you already live and change people's perspective on who you are. These can be frightening prospects because we invest our identities in these stories.

Remember, contemplation is a "long, loving look at the real." As we continue to practice gazing, what is most real will be revealed to us in new and deeper ways. We are drawn more deeply into the heart of the world. What is the story you are being invited to tell in this moment, in this frame? Is there a new story emerging? We discover a deeper call, which may demand that we step out of what is familiar.

The Art of Spiritual Discernment

> Listen to your life. See it for the fathomless mystery that it is. In the boredom and pain of it no less than in the excitement and gladness: touch, taste, smell your way to the holy and hidden heart of it because in the last analysis all moments are key moments and life itself is grace.
>
> **—Frederick Buechner**[1]

The root of the verb "discern" means discriminate; hence, in the Christian spiritual tradition, discernment refers to the *process of discriminating what is from God from what is not.*

Christians have been discerning from biblical times to the present, seeking to understand how God is present, acting, and calling—be it in personal prayer, in the worship of the faith community, through moral choices, or simply in the ebb and flow of ordinary life.

Discernment is the process of intentionally becoming aware of how God is present, active, and calling us as individuals and communities, so that we can respond with increasingly greater faithfulness.

Bringing discernment to our decision making means awakening and tutoring our ability to recognize what God desires for us in the moment. It means actively seeking God's call in the very process of making the decisions, big and small. We can bring this kind of active seeking into our photography as well, as we listen each moment to what is being offered to us in the moment.

Discernment is a way of listening deeply to the world around us and within us for God's voice and guidance. It is a way of being that encounters God in the center of our being and listens for the ways

God speaks to us from this center through God's desires for our own growing wholeness. In visio divina, we pay attention to images that shimmer forth to us and call us to see differently. We actively try to welcome in what we experience as both attractive and repulsive, so that we make sure to include all of the possible wisdom the world around us offers.

In the Emmaus story (Luke 24), it says that, as they were walking along the road with Jesus, even the disciples' "eyes were prevented from recognizing him." Discernment is about cultivating clarity of vision, which is where it connects so beautifully to the practice of contemplative photography. As we develop our ability to see through the lens, we grow in our capacity to see what is calling to us in the silent spaces.

Discernment is about foundational identity—how do I uniquely reveal the face of God? How do I uniquely love the world, while both recognizing and honoring my limits? Discernment also means what I am *not* called to do. When we frame an image with the camera, or a decision, we make choices about what to include and what to exclude. We can't include everything in our line of sight or commitment. Photography as a contemplative practice demands that we also make choices. Every time we look through the lens, we allow certain things into our frame of vision. The camera can offer us one school of discernment, a place to become more conscious of the choices we make.

Essential to the practice of discernment is learning when to say yes and when to say no. In this way, we frame and give limits to how we devote our energy. Often we are so eager to discover the deep yes of our lives that we forget the sacred practice of saying no. In a world that throws hundreds of invitations and demands our way, we may find ourselves with little energy for the things that bring us truly alive because we have invested in dozens of only moderately satisfying activities.

Contemplating the act of framing in photography can help illuminate the ways we need to frame our own lives, in terms of both the stories we tell and the ways we spend our energy. Paying attention to the decisions we make with each photograph can illuminate our own interior process of listening and making space. When I am receiving photos, am I so eager to "capture" everything around me that I miss being fully present to the moment? Or are there moments when I remember that this is a practice of saying both yes and no, of not "taking" everything around me but waiting to receive, to see what feels right and true.

Visual Discernment

Photography has sometimes been called the art of exclusion. The image is only meaningful because certain elements were included and others were kept out of the frame. You remove the elements that don't contribute to the emerging story. You keep out that which distracts the eye.

Much of the time when we choose to frame an image in a particular way, it is a largely intuitive process. I invite you to become more conscious of how this happens for you. Consider the ways the frame gives you visual clues and directs the eye in certain directions. Become curious about these choices you make when receiving photos without thinking it through too much. Hold these ideas gently, allowing them to just float across your awareness:

- **Vertical and horizontal:** Vertical framing draws the eye up and down, and horizontal framing draws attention from left to right. Notice which way you are intuitively drawn to hold your camera to receive a particular image.

- **Space between:** Whatever elements you include in your image relate to one another within that visual space and the space between things. The use of space and composition can be very evocative. There can be great power in trying to say one thing well. The discipline of the frame brings disparate elements together into a particular vision.

- **Cropping:** Another element of framing is cropping images. When something in a photo is cropped, it creates tension and a sense of mystery. There is a sense of the story spilling over the edges, and our imaginations move to wondering what has been concealed. Become aware of how you might crop a subject in your photo to see what effect this elicits in you in response.

- **Contrast:** *Anything we do to control or adjust an image becomes a frame.* Contrast is another tool in the framing of images. We explored shadow and light in the last chapter. Now, pay attention to the contrast between big and small, mechanical and natural, smooth and textured, warm and cool colors, focused and blurry, and recognizable and abstract elements.

Pause right now and take some time creating a square with your fingers and thumbs in front of you and use that frame as a way of simply exploring how the act of framing reveals and conceals, how it highlights and how it hides. Gaze around the room through this frame and notice what makes for interesting images. Notice where your eyes want to rest and what orientation feels satisfying. Notice what feels most freeing and life-giving. There is no right or wrong answer to this exploration; it is more about cultivating your own inner awareness.

Feel free to continue to play with framing in the digital processing stage. Most digital cameras and computers come with at least basic editing software where you can crop your images in different ways. Choose one image and try cropping it in two or three different ways (making sure to save an original image file), and notice what those choices evoke in you. Consider enhancing the color in an image or taking out the color altogether to create a black-and-white photo and see how it shifts the story being told. Experiment and play with seeing the image in different ways.

Other Elements of Composition

> Now to consult the rules of composition before making a picture is a little like consulting the law of gravitation before going for a walk. Such rules and laws are deduced from the accomplished fact; they are the products of reflection.
>
> **—Edward Weston**

While this book isn't about the technical aspects of photography, a brief look at composition can be a helpful way of learning some of the visual language of the art of photography. This is mainly what we are focusing on when we consider framing in the composition— what elements to include or not include as well as when to crop an image after we have received it. Sometimes it is helpful to know the "rules" we are working with so we can go ahead and break them.

There are six basic design elements when composing an image: line, shape, form, texture, pattern, and color. Most of these arise intuitively in photography as we discover what pleases our eye or feels satisfying.

Lines can be long or short, or thick or thin; lines are everywhere. Horizontal lines feel grounded and provide stability. We tend to scan the world from side to side. Think of a landscape image of a field or ocean and the felt experience of those lines. Vertical lines create a sense of lift and confidence, as do trees, tall buildings, and pillars. Consider the vertical and horizontal dimensions of our spiritual life, where the vertical dimension evokes a God who is transcendent, and the horizontal, one who is incarnational. Horizontal and vertical lines work together to form grids where your eye can rest and feel held. Both transcendence and immanence are necessary, but in a given image, we may be drawn to emphasize one or another. Lines can also be curved, like those of a sand dune or a shell. They can be diagonal, creating a sense of movement as they lead the eye across an image.

We identify objects in a two-dimensional image by their **shapes**, for example, if we photograph someone standing in front of the setting sun, we will see their silhouette or shape. **Form** is when the shape is extended into three dimensions and occurs in images where light gives something a sense of depth and substance.

Texture refers to the surface of a form and whether it is rough, smooth, uneven, or jagged. Think of paint peeling or rust flaking, walls crumbling, the smooth surface of shiny chrome on a car, and the roughness of tree bark. I love the beauty to be found in cracks and crevices; eyes of the heart invite us to see the holy in all of these places. Texture brings a tactile quality to your photos and also evokes emotion. Consider what feelings different textures evoke for you.

Pattern is found both in nature and in the human world, sometimes in an orderly, repetitive way and sometimes at random. Think of the intricate patterns of veins on leaves or the repeated spirals of a seashell. Railings and gates have their own patterns, along with wallpaper. Sometimes contemplating the amazing patterns in nature can evoke a sense of awe and become a prayer all on its own.

Color is something we will explore in its own chapter (chapter 5).

Some additional rules of composition include the "Rule of Thirds," which is a guideline commonly followed by visual artists. Imagine a grid of two horizontal lines and two vertical lines placed over an image to create nine equal sections. The idea is to place key parts of your composition on the lines and/or the four intersecting points where the lines cross.

The objective is to stop the subject and areas of interest (such as the horizon on a landscape) from bisecting the image, which happens when we center something, by placing them near one of the lines that would divide the image into three equal columns and rows, ideally near the intersection of those lines. The idea is that our eyes more naturally travel to one of these intersecting points. Play with this in your own photographic explorations, and see if your eye is naturally drawn to this principle and whether it enhances (or not) your sense of the sacred in an image.

The "Rule of Odds" focuses on the way groups of objects in odd numbers tend to be more compelling than in even numbers. Pay attention to photos of people, animals, shells, fruit, and so forth. Try photographing things in both evens and odds, and notice if each has a different quality or feeling to it for you. It may not, but it is always worth testing out these principles for yourself to see what you notice.

A final element to consider in the composition and framing of photographs is the use of **blur and focus**. Depth of field refers to the range of vision that appears acceptably sharp. You have seen images where just one small element is in focus while the rest of the photo moves into a gradual blur. This is another way to work with framing and highlighting something that is visually shimmering for you in a moment, an opening to a holy moment. The closer you are to something when you take a photo, generally the more shallow the depth of field is.

These technical principles are just one way of understanding the visual language of photography. They evolved as insights into how photography actually happens, rather than as predetermined rules to follow. When we are engaged in receiving images as a contemplative practice, we may or may not "follow the rules," but it can be helpful to notice how these principles are sometimes at work and offer us ways to make choices about what to give our focus to. Remember that, in framing, we are practicing visual discernment and becoming more present to the beauty being offered us in the moment. Notice your own relationship to "rules" and principles like these. Many of us live by too many rules already, especially when it comes to religious beliefs, which can hinder our creative exploration. If you notice yourself getting too caught up in trying to follow them, go for a walk with your camera where you intentionally try to break the photographic rules and see what you discover in that place of freedom.

Meditation:
Widening and Narrowing Your Gaze

In this meditation we will move into a quiet space in order to widen and focus our gaze. Through this meditation we discover that even as we are part of a big picture and our story is embedded in the wide narrative of family and culture, and of world events and nature, our story is also a unique expression of our being in this moment of time and space.

Find a comfortable position either seated or lying down. Begin by simply quieting yourself, and pay attention to your breathing. As you inhale, imagine God breathing life into you. As you exhale, allow yourself to experience a moment of release and surrender into this time and place, becoming fully present.

From this heart-centered place, become aware of your story. You are going to bring the eyes of your heart to a journey of the imagination, allowing yourself to gaze inwardly with compassion and curiosity. Allow your heart to fill with gratitude for the details of your unique unfolding in this world, trusting that your experiences have shaped you into who you are in this moment. Just be present to whatever stirs in you.

Breathing in and out again, widen your inner gaze to include your family members, close friends, companion animals, and members of your spiritual community. Take a few moments to honor the way these people and creatures are woven into the story of who you are and how they have shaped your life.

Widen your vision again to include the particular place where you live. How does the exterior landscape support or challenge your inner life? What are the characteristics or features of the place you inhabit, and how are they woven into your story?

Widen your gaze again to contemplate the culture in which you live. How does your life in this moment of the history of time shape your story? What is being called out from you in response to the lens of this time and place? Pause for a few moments here to notice what is stirring in you.

Continue to be aware of your breath, and this time, allow your inner gaze to widen and encompass the whole world. Be present to the way the global community is woven into your story. Imagine cultures and traditions across the earth all present at this very same moment of time.

Again, returning to your breath, widen your gaze to include the whole matrix of creation, all living creatures, plants and animals. Teilhard de Chardin described his vision of creation as the "breathing together of all things." Take a moment to inhale and exhale, and imagine the life-giving exchange that happens with plant life to sustain you moment by moment. Then imagine the breathing of living organisms in a rhythmic rise and fall across the planet. Be present to how your place in creation is connected to your story.

Allow your heart to open wide in gratitude for the ways all of these people and creatures and landscapes, across time and space, have shaped who you are right here and right now. Embrace the fullness of your own story as an expression of the intersection of all of these elements.

Connecting to your breath again, allow your inhale and exhale to begin to narrow your gaze back again while holding an awareness of the vast expanse in which you are embedded.

Then bring your focus back to your own heart. With your inner gaze, just take in this moment in time. Notice what you are experiencing right now after taking this interior journey. Reflect for a moment on your own unfolding story and all of the ways it is shaped. Gently connect with your breath, and return to the room ready to embark on a journey of a new way of seeing. Bring this awareness and expansiveness of seeing to your photographic process.

Photographic Exploration: Framing

Begin the photographic exploration for this theme by engaging in your contemplative walk, keeping in mind the theme of framing. Become aware of how you tell a story through your lens and the inclusion and exclusion of elements. Notice how framing with the camera helps to reveal and conceal, bring freedom and life or restrict them. Hold this awareness lightly as you practice being as fully present as you can, gazing with eyes of the heart, noticing what you discover in the process. Become aware of what is inviting you to pay attention and what story wants to be told. Receive each photo as part of an unfolding story that is being told about your own life. What do you discover in the process? Widen and narrow your frame.

PHOTOGRAPHIC EXPLORATION: EMPTINESS AND FULLNESS

Positive space refers to the subject of your image, while negative space—sometimes called "white space"—is everything else around it. Both are important. The negative space gives a place for the eye to rest. We might consider negative space as the silence that gives meaning to music and keeps it from sounding like a cacophony. The negative spaces of our own lives are those moments of rest and release from doing.

Experiment both with photographing empty spaces and also with filling your frame by eliminating all background. For example, pay attention to the sky and cloud formations; see what draws your

attention to the wide spaces. Or choose a subject in the distance, like a person standing in a field, and include them at the very edge of the image. How are they in relationship to the empty spaces? How does the empty space create a sense of rest or relationship to your subject?

Then notice something else in your life drawing you in, perhaps a flower or a friend. Let your subject fill the frame, making choices about what to crop out; you don't have to include the whole subject. How does this create a sense of intimacy with your subject? Notice the ways background clutter can distract you from what you want to focus on. How is this like your own life?

PHOTOGRAPHIC EXPLORATION: PERSPECTIVE

We generally hold the camera up to our eye and make images from eye level. But we can play with perspective by consciously looking

up, looking down, lying on the floor, or climbing up on a chair or ladder and receive images from this vantage point. See what you notice and discover by seeing the world from a new angle.

PHOTOGRAPHIC EXPLORATION: LINES, SHAPES, FORMS, TEXTURES, PATTERNS

Experiment with photographing just compositional elements as you find them. Make photographs emphasizing horizontal, vertical, diagonal, and curvy lines. Notice shapes of things rather than the things themselves. Photograph interesting textures and patterns.

Look below the surface of things as recognizable objects to which you bring certain expectations, and let yourself play with these elements on their own. Then spend some time with these images to notice what experience they evoke in you. How is your life like or unlike these elements?

PHOTOGRAPHIC EXPLORATION: WINDOWS AND DOORWAYS

Behold, I have left an open door before you which no one can close.

—Revelation 3:8

As you explore this chapter's theme, entertain the idea of a photo as a window. You don't look at the window frame itself; you look through it. We are not interested in the window itself. The opening reveals what is beyond. Depending on where you stand in relation to it, it will reveal different things. Depending on the time of day and the quality of light and the season, you will see different images. Pause and look out a window, just becoming aware of what it both reveals and conceals.

As you look through the viewfinder of your camera, become aware when there is a moment you want to lean into and look through or into (rather than at). What are the moments that call you inward or through?

Both doorways and windows are thresholds; they ask us to cross over, either physically with our body or our vision, or emotionally and spiritually to new inner territory. In her poem "When Death Comes," Mary Oliver writes, "I want to step through the door full of curiosity."[2] Explore how the frame of the camera invites you into deeper curiosity and discovery.

REFLECTION QUESTIONS

Naomi Shihab Nye has a beautiful poem titled "Valentine for Earnest Mann." In it, a man gives his wife two skunks as a valentine because he finds their eyes beautiful. This poem is about reframing what is normally seen as abhorrent into something beautiful. "Nothing was ugly / just because the world said so." Later in the poem she invites us to "re-invent whatever our lives give us" and find poetry hidden there—in the garage, the laundry, the mundane and ordinary elements of life.

- What are the skunks in your own shadow life that need some new stories where they become the Valentine's of your life, a love letter to the world from your whole self?

- Where do you discover the hidden poems of your life? Can you create visual poetry from the socks in your drawer or the pile of dirty dishes?

- What ordinary, everyday objects could be reinvented into a visual Valentine, expressing the beauty of the world hidden beneath our expectations?

- What are the boundaries your heart is longing to cross, seeking refreshment and repose? What is the frame you long to widen? How might your camera offer up insight into what that frame wants to contain?

- What are the new stories you have received through your photographic explorations that expand your sense of self? Which ones have offered the gift of focus and clarity?

5

THE SYMBOLIC SIGNIFICANCE OF COLOR

To be an artist it is not necessary to make a living from our creations. . . . To be an artist it is necessary to live with our eyes wide open, to breathe in the colors of mountain and sky, to know the sound of leaves rustling, the smell of snow, the texture of bark.

—Jan Phillips

If you pass by the color purple in a field and don't notice it, God gets real pissed off.

—Alice Walker

I understand how scarlet can differ from crimson because I know that the smell of an orange is not the smell of a grapefruit. I can also conceive that colors have shades and guess what shades are. In smell and taste there are variations not broad enough to be fundamental; so I call them shades. . . . The force of association drives me to say that white is exalted and pure, green is exuberant, red suggests love or shame or strength. Without the color or its equivalent, life to me would be dark, barren, a vast blackness.

—Helen Keller

Symbolic Significance of Color

Color is the stain of blackberry juice on the tips of your fingers after indulging in a mouthful of fresh-picked berries. It is the jeweled radiance of an autumn forest or a field of plump orange pumpkins. Color is the deep blue of sea and sky and the waves of emerald moss covering the trees of the Northwest.

From the grey days of winter to the brilliance of a bouquet of sunflowers, color can affect our mood and spirit. We are deeply affected by color, and develop most and least favorite colors. Some of us care about how we understand ourselves in relation to color, and we employ the industries designed to "match your color" so that our wardrobe can presumably complement our skin tone best. When we paint a room, we intuitively understand that whatever color we choose will changes its mood. And we respond to the moods of color around us: when it's bright outside, we often put on brighter clothing in summer to reflect the world around us.

Remember how the classic movie *The Wizard of Oz* begins in the dusty plains of Kansas in black and white to emphasize this world without color in which Dorothy lives? When she lands in Oz, the world becomes vibrant with rainbow shades, dazzling in its sheer variety of hues. By the end of the film, when Dorothy returns home, her Kansas world is also depicted in color. Why? Because her own eyes have been opened to the possibilities there.

Colors are related to every aspect of our lives—our clothes, our entertainment, our food, and our rooms—and not surprisingly color plays a significant role in Christian tradition. In early martyr tradition, Christians killed for their beliefs were called "red martyrs." Red indicated the violence they suffered and the blood that was shed.

Once Christianity became a widespread religion, red martyrdom no longer occurred, so those who committed themselves without bloodshed to a holy and ascetic life, forsaking the comforts of the world, were sometimes referred to as "white martyrs." White symbolized their purity and dedication to God.[1]

Later, in Ireland, where Christianity was introduced without bloodshed, there were "green martyrs" who left the comforts of home to go off into the green wilderness to live a holy life. They followed the example of the early desert monks who fled to the harsh landscapes to focus on God.

Colors also play a significant role in religious art, especially icon symbolism. Colors become a symbolic language pointing to different qualities of the Saints depicted.

The color blue is often associated with the Virgin Mary to emphasize her title as Queen of Heaven and is associated with heaven and the mystery of the mystical life. Blue often appears in the vestments of Christ and the apostles as well.

Gold is used in icons to symbolize the divine light. The Hebrew word *aour*, meaning "light," is similar to the Latin word *aurum*, meaning "gold." In illuminated manuscripts, gold is also used to express the radiance of the divine. I like to imagine those ancient monks being out in a sunlit forest, the trees luminous and glowing, and returning to their scriptoriums to see if they could capture a little of what they experienced on parchment.

One of the most frequently used colors in icons is red: the color of heat, passion, and love. It is the color of blood and the torment that Christ endured. Saints depicted in red garments symbolize blood shed for faith and a passion for God exacting the price of a life.

Other colors in icons, like purple, are associated with royalty; white, with purity or innocence. Green points to the fecundity of the earth and brown with humility (a color we recognize in simple undyed monastic robes).

It is not only saints and significant figures of faith who have associative colors. In denominations with liturgical traditions, each season also has a symbolic color. Ordinary time is represented by green to symbolize new life and growth. Advent is connected with the color blue; Lent is purple. The seasons of Christmas and Easter are connected to the color white, and black is reserved for solemn occasions like Good Friday or the offices of the dead.

Color speaks a symbolic language and elicits strong associations for us. And this is a language and palette we can pay attention to in our photography as well.

Viriditas and the Greening Power of God

> Opus Verbi viriditas / The work of the Word is greenness.
>
> **—Hildegard of Bingen**

> There is nothing in creation that does not have some radiance—either greenness or seeds or flowers, or beauty—otherwise it would not be part of creation.
>
> **—Hildegard of Bingen**

> And how would God be known as the Eternal One if brilliance did not emerge from God? For there is no creature without some kind of radiance—whether it be greenness, seeds, buds, or another kind of beauty.
>
> **—Hildegard of Bingen**

Hildegard of Bingen

Hildegard of Bingen, the twelfth-century Benedictine abbess, offers us another example of the deep spiritual significance a color can have. *Viriditas* is the Latin noun for "greenness" and is derived from *vivere*, meaning "to become or be green" and indicating vitality, fecundity, lushness, verdure, or growth. Hildegard used the term to describe the greening power of God, the animating life force within all creation that gives it life, moisture, and vitality. *Viriditas* is the life energy that brings fullness to human beings in our quest to become more truly our authentic selves. It indicates vigor, fertility, and health. *Viriditas* is not just the property of what we would normally think of living things but also the property of such inanimate objects as rocks. The natural world is not simply inert but filled with life and power.

Hildegard describes the "green finger of God," indicating that this vitality is a manifestation of God's activity in the world. The life that suffuses the world flows forth from God who is "the highest and fiery power" and "has kindled every living spark" (DW 1.2). *Viriditas* is Hildegard's singular idea to illuminate the dynamic interconnectedness and intercommunion of all levels of created life with each other and with God as Source. Her emphasis on greenness symbolizes the inner dynamism of life in all its burgeoning growth, vibrancy, freshness, and fecundity as emanating from the life-creating and sustaining power of God.

Through this highly symbolic word, viridity, Hildegard harmoniously interweaves all created life—cosmic, human, angelic, and celestial—with God. Greenness encompasses not only the cosmos but also angelic life in its mirroring of God's life, fecundity, creativity, and harmony. We might say that *viriditas* is God's love, energizing the world, and making it living and fruitful. Nothing exists without *viriditas* because nothing exists without God loving it and wanting it to exist. For Hildegard, the universality of greenness shows us the universality of God's love.

Hildegard brought both a physical and spiritual understanding to a specific color, and brought a deep and meaningful symbolism to our experience of green. When we begin to open our own eyes to the profound meaning and effect color can have on us and our connection to virtues and values, we train our eyes to see this other layer of significance in what we see all the time. Our camera, then, becomes a portal again to assist us in finding color's power all around us. When you look through the frame, what colors are at play, and what effect do they have on your own spirit?

For Hildegard of Bingen, *viriditas* wasn't just something evident in creation but also reflective of the very state of our soul. We each have the capacity to bring forth new life just as the earth brings forth greenness. Becoming more aware of the quality of greenness of the earth helps support our personal discernment about where we are being called toward new growth and where we experience aridity that needs God's moist breath.

Color is an important element in both the art and prayer of photography, even in black-and-white images. We are encouraged to cultivate an appreciation for the symbolic power of various colors for us, and which ones seem to shimmer most strongly. As we develop "eyes of the heart," we begin to see how color speaks a language all of its own, with the camera helping to reveal its power.

MEDITATION:
VIRIDITY AND ARIDITY

For Hildegard of Bingen, the fecund greenness of the earth is a visual indication of health and flourishing, while the opposite experience is *ariditas* or dryness of earth and spirit. Contemplative practice can sharpen our eyes so that we become more keenly aware of the presence or absence of greenness in our lives and the world around us. I invite you to pause here for a few moments and center yourself, quieting your mind and thoughts, and resting into your heart. Then, when you feel you have found a place of stillness, read through the story of Ezekiel and the dry bones in a slow and contemplative way:

> The hand of the LORD came upon me, and he brought me out by the spirit of the LORD and set me down in the middle of a valley; it was full of bones. He led me all around them; there were very many lying in the valley, and they were very dry. He said to me, "Mortal, can these bones live?" I answered, "O Lord GOD, you know." Then he said to me, "Prophesy to these bones, and say to them: O dry bones,

hear the word of the LORD. "Thus says the Lord GOD to these bones: I will cause breath to enter you, and you shall live. I will lay sinews on you, and will cause flesh to come upon you, and cover you with skin, and put breath in you, and you shall live; and you shall know that I am the LORD." So I prophesied as I had been commanded; and as I prophesied, suddenly there was a noise, a rattling, and the bones came together, bone to its bone. I looked, and there were sinews on them, and flesh had come upon them, and skin had covered them; but there was no breath in them. Then he said to me, "Prophesy to the breath, prophesy, mortal, and say to the breath: Thus says the Lord GOD: Come from the four winds, O breath, and breathe upon these slain, that they may live." I prophesied as he commanded me, and the breath came into them, and they lived, and stood on their feet, a vast multitude. Then he said to me, "Mortal, these bones are the whole house of Israel. They say, 'Our bones are dried up, and our hope is lost; we are cut off completely.' Therefore prophesy, and say to them, Thus says the Lord GOD: I am going to open your graves, and bring you up from your graves, O my people; and I will bring you back to the land of Israel. And you shall know that I am the LORD, when I open your graves, and bring you up from your graves, O my people. I will put my spirit within you, and you shall live, and I will place you on your own soil; then you shall know that I, the LORD, have spoken and will act," says the LORD.

—Ezekiel 37:1–14

Breathe in those images, and ponder how they are speaking to you in this moment of your life.

Imagine where in your life you experience this kind of brokenness, dryness, and complete lack of nourishment or anything to sustain you. "Our bones are dried up, and our hope is lost." Does any part of your being resonate with this image? Where do you experience aridity? What are the dry bones of your life? Where have you become depleted in your service to others? See if you can visualize the scene before you. If you had your camera with you, what kind of images might be received?

Welcome in whatever arises in your reflection with compassion and gentleness. Hold these dry and arid places with loving awareness.

Then imagine that you can call on the Great Breath to infuse you with life. Imagine, with Hildegard, that there is a great source of greenness and fecundity at the foundation of the world and you can invite this sacred presence to fill your being with this life-giving greening power. With each inhale, imagine that you are inviting in this moist and verdant energy into your body, and then your mind, your emotions, and your spirit. As you exhale, imagine letting go of the dryness, breathing it out, releasing its hold on you. Again, visualize this scene and imagine what kind of photographic images might be received from this experience.

Notice how the visual quality of this potent color green feels in your body. Rest here for a while, savoring this experience and the felt connection with this color of life.

Gently return from this space of inner reflection to the room. Allow some time for journaling to note what came up for you in the process.

PHOTOGRAPHIC EXPLORATION: FOLLOWING A COLOR

Choose a single color to focus on, perhaps your favorite color, or maybe your least favorite. Maybe it is a color whose qualities you want to draw into your life, like red for passion, white for purity, or green for fecundity. Or you could begin your walk and notice which color is drawing your attention the most.

Now, go on a contemplative walk, receiving a series of photos that focus on this single color and the way it appears in different scenes and objects.

After you have returned from your contemplative walk, look through the new set of photographs or perhaps through earlier ones, and create a sequence of photos highlighting your chosen color. Notice if there is a pattern forming in the images received and whether they tell a story.

PHOTOGRAPHIC EXPLORATION:
COLOR SPECTRUM

For this exploration, choose a particular kind of object to focus on, for example, shoes or signs. Go for a walk, and see if you can find this object in a whole range of colors—at least in the primary colors of red, blue, and yellow. Then search out orange, purple, and green. Add in black and white if you are feeling ambitious. Create a series of photos of consistent subjects in an array of colors. Have some fun with this process.

PHOTOGRAPHIC EXPLORATION:
BLACK AND WHITE

In addition to exploring color through photography, reducing a palette to black and white is another choice we can make for our images.

If you have a camera or smartphone that offers a black-and-white setting as you receive images or that allows you to convert them to black and white in postprocessing on your computer, spend some time with that palette. Notice which images look more intriguing or inviting in black and white.

Black and white usually creates more of a sense of starkness and can be especially powerful in images that don't have a lot of shading and gradations. I love the feeling of these photos; they seem to reveal the essence of an image in ways that color doesn't. Winter trees look especially powerful in black and white.

REFLECTION QUESTIONS

- Which colors seem to energize you, and which ones drain you? Do you notice any patterns?

- Do the symbolic associations with different colors have resonance for you?

- If your life were a mosaic of different colored tiles, what elements would the different colors represent?

- What effect does black and white create for you? How does your spirit respond to black-and-white images?

- What are you noticing and discovering about the impact of color in your life?

- If you could describe the presence of God only in terms of color, which colors would be most significant?

6

WHAT IS MIRRORED BACK?

Only by going alone in silence, without baggage, can one truly get into the heart of the wilderness. The spiritual eye sees not only rivers of water but of air. It sees the crystals of the rock in rapid sympathetic motion, giving enthusiastic obedience to the sun's rays, then sinking back to rest in the night. The whole world is in motion to the center. I only went out for a walk, and finally concluded to stay out till sundown, for going out, I found, was really going in.

—John Muir

And now here is my secret, a very simple secret:
It is only with the heart that one can see clearly;
What is essential is invisible to the eye.
—Antoine de Saint-Exupery

When I gaze with open eyes
at what you, my God, have created here,
heaven is already mine.
—Hildegard of Bingen

"Reflections"

Looking for myself,
I creep from one reflection to the next.
I stare, I see
suggestions of my son, my granddaughter.
I'm not there,

though if I should bend this way, and this
couldn't I curve back to the place
where the first mirror surely held me
in perfect, infinite, loving regard?

I'm drawn to any gleaming surface
—the polished floor, a silver horn,
windows in a revolving door.
They're never right, never
that milk-blue light I'm longing for.
Often I'm only smudges,
or scattered by cracks;
but I'm there at least,
I've some hold on the ground inhabited
before I found out what I lacked
and what the mirror did.
And what the mirror
did.

—Carole Satyamurti [1]

Have you ever caught a glimpse of yourself in a mirror in a way that surprised you or allowed you to see something differently? Reflections offer us another window into seeing the world more deeply by changing our perspective and turning things upside down. You are invited to continue your photographic explorations while holding lightly your work with shadow and light and your work with framing, and being aware of these tools of the art of photography.

As in color, our focus on reflections moves us to consider the specific *content* of our images rather than the medium or photographic tools, directly. First we begin with looking. You may discover images reflected in a mirror or a window, in a puddle or lake, or in the chrome of a car or a polished floor. Be attentive to those places where images are offered in repetition or reflection, mirrored back to you, and what they invite you to ponder.

Through shadow and light we have contemplated our unclaimed inner energies and lives and then moved to consider the way we frame those and the new stories we are invited to tell about them. Through color we have explored the visual, emotional, and symbolic impact color can have on us. In this chapter, however, you are invited to consider seeing from another point of view. Reflections offer us another way of receiving the gift of new eyes. We return to the image of seeing with the eyes of the heart and bring this perspective to what is revealed when we are gifted with our own reflection. You might say a reflection is a seeing within seeing.

Mirrors don't just offer back a literal reflection—depending on the mirrored surface, the image may be reflected through bends or cracks, through translucence or opaque colors, or through shiny or dull surfaces. The qualities of these mirrors invite us to consider the ways the world sees us and how we might continue to be invited to new perspectives of ourselves. Mirrors can also distort our perceptions of how something looks.

The images you receive may not just be reflections of you; they may also be reflections of other things or persons that invite you to consider their meaning and significance for your life. Allow each reflection to become a symbol for something in you to ponder.

In your work with photography as a contemplative practice, and throughout this book, you have been invited to see with the eyes of the heart—gazing upon the world and gazing upon yourself to witness to the truth revealed there. In David Whyte's poem "All the True Vows," using the metaphor of water, he invites us to remember the truth at our own center and then "whisper that truth / to the quiet reflection" found in a lake. There is something powerful about speaking aloud as we see our own face, an act of visual prayer and reverence for who we were created to be. The camera helps us to see this truth more clearly and in the act of receiving an image, we are validating the truth of it for our own experience. You might even want to take a journey to the edge of the water—a lake or seashore or puddle nearby, or even run a bath and lean over the edge of the tub—and whisper your truth to that "quiet reflection" you find there, listening for the response and remembering it. Then sing it aloud in your own voice, create a melody or chant, and repeat those verses to yourself in quiet moments.

Mystical Mirrors

The metaphor of the mirror was an important one in Christian mystical tradition, especially during the medieval period. The understanding was that all of creation was a reflection of the divine but it becomes clouded. As early as St. Paul's famous line "For now we see in a mirror, dimly, but then we will see face to face" (1 Corinthians 13:12), we meet the metaphor of the mirror. In Paul's day, the Roman era, mirrors were polished brass; only later in the Renaissance were they made from clear glass.

The goal of the spiritual journey is to polish this mirror, to make its reflection clearer. We find this image of the "polished mirror" in Sufism as well. The poet Rumi writes, "Everyone sees the Unseen in proportion to the clarity of his heart, and that depends upon how much he has polished it. Whoever has polished it more sees more—more Unseen forms become manifest to him."[2] Sufism uses the analogy of the human heart being like a polished mirror that reflects the light of the divine. The more polished our heart is, the more of the divine can be reflected.

Unfortunately, our hearts are usually covered with dust and rust so not as much of the divine can be reflected through us. This opaqueness is our lower unconscious, our shadow side, all those parts of ourselves that we'd rather pretend do not exist. Our job is to polish our hearts so more of the divine attributes can shine through us. Think of times when your camera lens has become coated with grime, or the internal workings have become dusty, so that the images coming through have lost their shimmer or brightness. I have to bring my camera into a repair shop every few months to have it professionally cleaned, so that my instrument of vision offers me as much clarity as possible.

In Jewish tradition, the Book of Wisdom offers a similar insight into the power of mirrors. Lady Wisdom is described as "a reflection of eternal light, / a spotless mirror of the working of God, / and an image of his goodness" (Wisdom 7:26).

In the book of her life, Carmelite mystic Teresa of Avila writes,

> My soul suddenly became recollected; and it seemed to me to be like a brightly polished mirror, without any part on the back or sides or top or bottom that wasn't totally clear. In its center Christ our Lord was shown to me, in the way I usually see Him. It seemed to me I saw him clearly in every part of my soul, as though in a mirror. And this mirror also . . . was completely engraved upon the Lord Himself by means of a very loving communication I wouldn't know how to describe.[3]

Teresa goes on to write about the ways our humanness and brokenness clouds this mirror "with mist, leaving it black," so God cannot be revealed or seen. Even in our photography, we do not receive photos directly of God; rather, we receive images that point to something beyond us, or something beneath the surface of our expectations. Our photos can become mirrors to a clearer vision of God, just as we ourselves are called to become a clear reflection of the one who is our Source.

Mechthild of Magdeburg, a Beguine mystic, describes God as the "eternal mirror" into which we gaze; however, our vision is clouded. The soul is the inner mirror that reflects the divine light: "[The soul] says: 'Lord, You are my loved one, my desire, my flowing fountain, my sun and I am Your mirror.'"[4]

To connect us briefly back to some of the previous themes—our own internal mirrors become obscured by shadows we reject. The camera helps us to turn our gaze onto these subjects we would prefer to keep hidden. When we pay attention to how we frame something, we discover what we value most and also what we want to turn away from. The purpose of bringing these to our attention is so that we can become more aware of what we deny as sacred or having value. The camera as a clear mirror can reflect this back to us. When we receive images from a whole spectrum of subjects and themes, and become aware of the ways we tend to narrowly focus on certain things, we begin to expand our capacity to see.

We meet reflections and mirrors throughout history and throughout our cultural stories. Alice went through the looking glass to an alternate world. In fairy tales mirrors can be signs of vanity, like the queen in Snow White asking her daily question of who is the fairest in the land. The magical mirror in this tale does not simply reflect what is in front of it however but also gives voice to the unseen; it speaks the truth of what can and cannot be seen. It is also brutally honest and unwavering. The magic mirror cannot be deceived.

Mirrors can distort, but they can also reflect back truth; they can reveal reality to us. They can help us to see more clearly by presenting another way of seeing things. When we have cultivated our gifts of discernment, the mirror can become a reflection of what is most sacred.

The camera can function as a lens and mirror with which to see the world more clearly. Traditional SLR cameras all used mirrors to create images as part of how they operated. When we receive an image, we have the opportunity to cultivate our ability to see what is really there and not only what we want to see in a given scene. Photography can help to reflect back the truth to us.

When we allow ourselves to see things from a new perspective, which is what a mirror and our camera can offer, or when we allow ourselves to be surprised by God, we find ourselves on what the monastic tradition calls the path of conversion. Conversion is a commitment to ongoing growth and means we have never fully arrived in this lifetime but are always deepening and exploring the inner journey toward God. It also means that when we grow cynical about life or think we have seen it all, our commitment to conversion has grown clouded. As we develop our ability to see with the "eyes of the heart," and see the world more fully as it is, we need clear lenses, polished mirrors, and other ways of focusing and heightening our vision. These have the capacity to serve us in our ongoing conversion as we keep discovering there are always more layers of illusion to break through.

The way to go about polishing our inner mirror is through spiritual practice and cultivating our capacity to see God more clearly in more places and experiences.

MEDITATION: POLISHING YOUR HEART'S MIRROR

Find a comfortable seated position and begin to settle into the silence. Turn your gaze inward, closing your eyes, and imagine you are stepping across a threshold into your inner landscape. Begin to draw your breath more deeply. As you inhale welcome in this gift of life, sustaining you moment by moment. As you exhale, release and surrender whatever thoughts or distractions are not needed during this time of meditation. Move through several cycles of breath with this rhythm of embracing and releasing.

Gently draw your awareness from your head, down into your heart center, perhaps placing a hand on your heart to make a physical connection with your body. Rest for a moment there, noticing what you are feeling, making space for whatever your experience is without trying to change it. Then drawing on the infinite source of compassion that the mystics tell us is present in our hearts, let yourself fill with compassion for yourself and your experience, holding yourself gently and tenderly.

Resting in this heart space, imagine you can look into your own heart and see a mirror there. Notice what this mirror looks like. What material is it made of? Perhaps brass or silver, tin or glass, or something else altogether. Notice the quality of its surface. Is it clouded or rusty? Opaque or obscured? Shiny or gleaming? Coated with dust or grit? Be with whatever it is you discover there, holding it with compassion.

Enter into a time of dialogue with this inner mirror. What is it that keeps me from reflecting the divine radiance? Listen for the response. How might I polish and shine this mirror?

When you have finished exploring this image, return to your breath. Take several gentle inhales and exhales, and then slowly let your breath return your awareness to the room. Allow some time to be with your experience, perhaps journaling about the images you encountered, or using drawing materials to reflect what you saw there.

Photographic Exploration: Mirrors

Engage in your contemplative walk and photographic journey, paying attention to reflections and receiving images mirrored back to you. Notice reflections in chrome, windows, on water, and in surprising places. See if you can heighten your awareness of the ways the world is reflecting itself back to you. Let the mirrors you find reflect

things as they are and offer you new perspectives. Notice the way some mirrors seem to distort while others help to focus.

Become aware of what is inviting you to pay attention and what you notice stirring in you in response. Receive each invitation as a gift and as a catalyst for your own reflection and inner growth. How does this image reveal new things to you, new perspectives about who you are or who God is?

PHOTOGRAPHIC EXPLORATION: REFLECTIONS ON WATER

If you live near a body of water, whether a lake, river, sea, pond, or even a reflecting pool, go down to it on a breezy or windy day and make photos of the reflections in the ripples of the water's surface. Play with different angles, exploring how the distortion of the water creates different kinds of images.

Then return on a day when the wind is calm and the air is still. Make photos of the reflections in the smooth surface of the water, and notice the difference between this experience and the other one. What do you notice about the capacity for reflections in stillness and in agitation?

Photographic Exploration: Reflecting Virtues

One way we can bring the mirroring capacity of our cameras more intentionally into our process is to seek out images in the world that reflect something we want to cultivate in ourselves. One of the traditions in Christian spirituality, rather than focusing on our flaws and shortcomings, is to practice cultivating certain virtues such as patience, generosity, or compassion. Consider which virtue you would like to integrate into your own life and make a commitment to focus on it for the next several days. On your contemplative walks, hold this virtue in your heart, and ask to receive images that reflect

it and reveal new aspects of it to you. Pay attention to what you encounter. Let your photos offer a reflection of this virtue—a window into seeing it from a new perspective. Sometimes trying to focus on developing patience feels like an abstract notion. But if we discover the beauty in a snail moving ever so slowly across the earth, that moment of image can remain in us as a powerful reflection of what we seek in our own lives.

PHOTOGRAPHIC EXPLORATION: REFLECTING POETRY

This is a similar exercise to the one above, except that our focus here is on poetry. There are books such as *A Year with C. S. Lewis* or *A Year with Rumi* that provide daily readings for the year from a beloved

poet or author. Take on a daily practice of reading a poem or inspirational quote and then holding it with you throughout the day in a kind of slow and extended lectio divina. As you move through your day, be aware of images that connect with what you read, offering a new dimension to it. You can move through the same process with daily scripture readings.

REFLECTION QUESTIONS

- What is your relationship to mirrors? In our culture we have different kinds of stories about mirrors—sometimes they point to vanity, sometimes people "endow" them with cultural meeting: if you break one there is seven years of bad luck. In the Jewish tradition of sitting shiva, mirrors are covered to focus on the person who has died, and to not focus on your own reflection. Spend some time becoming aware of how your mirrors impact you in both positive and negative ways. Take a few moments to quiet your spirit and ask for insight into your relationship with mirrors, and see if images, feelings, or memories emerge. Just naming these can help release resistance that may arise.

- What did you discover about yourself by paying attention to the way things are reflected? What did this reverse perspective offer as a gift to you?

- In Carole Satyamurti's poem at the beginning of this chapter, she describes the mirror that holds her in "perfect, infinite, loving regard." How might the reflections you receive be a way to receive the world in loving regard—with eyes of the heart?

- What are the mirrors being lifted to you? Are there moments when the mirror reflected back your grief or your joy?

7
—

DISCOVERING THE HOLY
WITHIN US

With an eye made quiet by the power of harmony
And the deep power of joy
We see into the life of things

—William Wordsworth

I become a transparent eyeball; I am nothing; I see all: the currents of the Universal Being circulate through me; I am part and parcel of God.

—Ralph Waldo Emerson

Nobody sees a flower—really—it is so small. We haven't time—and to see takes time, like to have a friend takes time.

—Georgia O'Keeffe

Self-Portraits

In the first two chapters, we began by simply practicing the art of receiving images out in the world, being present to the gifts offered to us for our own inner exploration. Then in chapter 3 we began to dive into the different dimensions of sacred seeing through the lens and focused on the interplay of shadow and light within, followed by chapter 4 with an exploration of how we frame (and reframe) our lives and the stories we tell about ourselves. Chapter 5 then invited us to consider the inspiration of color, and chapter 6 offered ways of seeing how the holy is reflected in the world.

Each of these themes weaves a thread and leads us to this chapter on self-portraits. Here, I invite you to consider what it means to see and *be seen* by others. In revealing ourselves directly in this way through our photos, there is often a great sense of vulnerability. In some sense, all the photos you have received already in this process are self-portraits, as they each reveal something about what moves you.

As you engage in the process, again be very aware of your internal process; notice where your resistance arises and where you enter into a state of flow. Be curious about what this theme prompts in you. Bring more awareness to your inner dialogue, and allow it to bring some insight to the process for you. How might you create a self-portrait that expresses some of the conversation that happens inside of you as you contemplate how to go about this project?

Gazing upon ourselves is an act of great intimacy. It is especially intimate to receive these images of ourselves with the eyes of the heart. Before you begin, make sure to breathe deeply and connect with your heart's awareness so that you can gaze upon yourself with compassion and the desire for deeper awareness and understanding.

True Self and False Self

Every one of us carries an illusory persona: a false self. As we have been exploring, we are not very good at seeing through illusion. Our vision becomes clouded over by cultural expectations and personal striving and goals. Just as we do not see the world around us as it really is, neither do we see ourselves in this light. We spend much of our energy devoted to maintaining this mask, without ever letting others know who we really are and what we most deeply desire. We keep this so hidden that we ourselves also forget the truth. So spiritual practice becomes a lifetime journey of uncovering what is hidden.

What we call sin is an assumption that my false self is the fundamental reality around which everything else is centered. People might spend their whole lives striving for power, achievements, and possessions that build up the strength of the false self. We perpetuate the false self in our art-making, when we seek to create only images beautiful in the eyes of others or photos that are "marketable" rather than truthful.

The emotions of the false self are constantly changing—up, then down, and then up again. We are carried by the waves of surface experience and feeling. When we drop down into the true self, we discover a place of equanimity and calm that does not get hooked or swept away by every mood. We may touch this experience in the midst of a photographic exploration, where suddenly the frantic grasping of our mind stills and we discover an unexpected stillness in the midst of creating.

If we are lucky, one day we will encounter the limits of this way of living. We will start to ask questions of deeper meaning, of what really matters. The striving and clinging begins to fall away, much like the veils of illusion that slowly fall from in front of our eyes. We will let our photographs reflect the full spectrum of the world around us.

To discover who I really am, my true self or nature, I have to give up my own plans for myself and listen deeply for the desires that God planted in my heart. I must discover who I am beneath the accolades and achievements.

The essence of the contemplative life helps us to encounter and act from this true self, while slowly letting go of the promptings of our false or superficial self. Each of us is actually made up of a multitude of identities. When we live from the false self, we want to uplift those parts of our being that elicit praise from others while submerging those that don't fit in with our self-image. This is the shadow material we explored previously.

The journey toward wholeness is always to welcome in all of ourselves, and in this act of hospitality, we slowly integrate the different voices within us competing for attention. We learn to live out of the unity of voices that we are. The images we receive through our camera lens help us to begin to see the richness and diversity of the world around us, and so we might begin to see this within as well.

Thomas Merton wrote in *The Inner Experience*:

> The worst thing that can happen to a person who is already divided up into a dozen different compartments is to seal off yet another compartment and tell him that this one is more important than all others, and that he must henceforth exercise a special care in keeping it separate from them. . . . The first thing you have to do, before you start thinking about such a thing as contemplation, is to try to recover your basic natural unity, to reintegrate your compartmentalized being into a coordinated and simple whole, and learn to live as a unified human person. This means that you have to bring back together the fragments of your distracted existence so that when you say "I" there is really someone present to support the pronoun you have uttered.[1]

To find our true self-portrait, however, is a challenging road to travel because it means renouncing the false self with all of its ingrained patterns and habits, and all of the affirmations it receives, letting go of the comforts and securities of all that is familiar and setting out on a journey toward what is unknown to ourselves—who we most truly and deeply are. We cling again and again to our familiar ways of being and relating with others.

This true self is not an idealized self, or a perfect self, but rather the unadorned, vulnerable, human self we all contain. There is no compulsive striving for attention and affirmation.

Worthy of Being Seen

Self-portraits can bring up a lot of emotion. I know, for myself, I resist being the subject of photos. In part, this is because growing up, as an only child and first grandchild in a family where everyone owned a camera, I was the focus of the camera's gaze so often. Now that I am an adult, I appreciate the choice not to be seen in this sometimes one-dimensional or limited-dimensional way. However, there is also an invitation for me to be gentler with myself and explore the discomfort that this brings up for me.

Many of us have issues with being seen, fully, by ourselves and by the world around us. If this is true of you, then this chapter may be the most important and tender in the whole book for you. Sitting with your sense of vulnerability and self-doubt, in a world that judges attractiveness based on very narrow parameters, is an act of courage: looking through the photos we receive of ourselves, being in a compassionate way with the judgments that come up, and practicing gentleness with ourselves.

Some of these images may surprise you. You might discover some where you like the way you look, some where you look more tired than you thought you did, or some where a family resemblance is revealed.

The act of making and receiving self-portraits through the photograph is, in essence, a way of saying "look at me." When we hear messages about vanity and not being too full of ourselves, we hold back.

Of course, every photo we make is in some way a self-portrait, because it reveals something about how we see the world. Begin here perhaps, exploring what your photos have to say about you. As you summon up courage to get in front of the lens, rather than just behind it, go slowly. Share your images with people who love and support you whole-heartedly.

Dialogue with Your Images

There is a technique in Gestalt psychotherapy that uses an empty chair to explore unresolved feelings and issues from the past. People are asked to imagine someone specific in that empty chair and to engage that someone in dialogue. Sometimes, they are asked to assume both sides of the dialogue—both the person represented by the empty chair and themselves. The idea is that, when we engage in true dialogue with something or someone we experience conflict with, we grow in our compassion for ourselves and others.

Find an image of yourself that makes you uncomfortable. Sit with it, trying to release judgment and just opening a space for receiving. Imagine that this image is a different identity and you can have a dialogue with it. Give it a voice and enter into conversation. You might do this through writing or in your imagination.

You could also do this exercise by becoming aware of inner conflicting voices. Perhaps there is an inner perfectionist who always wants to get things right and at the same time there is an inner adventurer who is ready to take a step into the unknown, without any idea of the outcome. Often in this space between voices we experience a lot of tension. Go on a contemplative walk, and see if you can receive an image that represents each of these parts of self. Then when you return home, let the images enter into dialogue with each other. Let them speak from the first person. What do they have to say to one another?

This is part of the journey of integration and wholeness when we embrace our inner multitude.

MEDITATION:
BODY GRATITUDE

The purpose of this meditation is to move you deeply into an awareness of your body and into a sense of gratitude for all your body has
offered to you.[2] The act of engaging in self-portraits often brings up
all of our insecurities and inner chatter about our bodies, and this
meditation helps move you into a place of compassion and thank-
fulness. You might consider engaging the meditation before your
self-portrait session to become more aware of the stories your body
carries. Then your photography comes from a place of appreciation,
gratitude, and longing for discovery, rather than anxiety or fear.

I invite you to be open to what you may discover through the
process. We each carry with us so much history that is literally em-
bodied in our physical selves. Our bodies have carried us through
joys and heartbreaks and are the vessels through which we experience the world.

You might want to experience this meditation before you begin
your photographic journey as a way to ground yourself in your body
and in a sense of spaciousness and receptivity.

Prepare yourself for moving inward by tending to your breath
and to your heart. Put your hands over your heart and give thanks
for the wonder of this blood that pumps through your body; give
thanks for the breath that infuses you. Take a moment to honor these
automatic rhythms that sustain life.

Move your awareness more deeply into your body. Ground yourself in the wisdom of your body, listening as closely as you can.

Gently move your awareness into your feet and notice what you
feel. Take a few moments to offer thanks for the many ways your
feet have served and supported you. Become aware of any memories
that rise up, and take time to be present to them. Reflect on how you
experience yourself being rooted in the earth. Allow any feelings or

images that want to arise to have space to move within you. (Allow some time for this.) Breathe in gratitude and exhale release.

For each area of the body invite gratitude in and notice any memories or images that are stirred. Spend a few moments contemplating the question for each one.

> Legs: How do you stand in the world? How do you walk in the world?
> Pelvis: What are you giving birth to in the world?
> Belly: What nourishes you?
> Chest and Heart: Whom do you love?
> Back: What are you carrying?
> Arms: What do you embrace?
> Throat: What wants to be spoken or sung?
> Face: What is the face you show to the world?

Bring your awareness back to the whole of your body. Hold these questions: What is your body trying to teach you? What questions is your body asking? What are your body's invitations? What kind of wisdom does your body offer you today? Where has your body failed you? Is there forgiveness you are invited to offer?

Close your time by bringing a sense of gratitude for what has been revealed. Now slowly bring your awareness back to the room. Take a few moments to write down anything you noticed, any stories or memories that emerged, and transition yourself gently back.

Photographic Exploration:
Self-Portrait

As you consider receiving self-portraits, you may be thinking of a traditional image of your face (which may indeed be how some of these are received). However, bring what you have already learned to this process—self-portraits can be done by playing with shadow and light, they can use creative framing so only a part of yourself is revealed, and they can be done through reflection in water, a mirror, a window, or some other shiny surface that reveals something of who you are. You could make a photo of just a part of your body—a foot, a hand, or an eye. There are also what are known as "environmental

self-portraits," where you reveal something about yourself through significant objects in your environment.

If you have a timer on your camera, you can play with receiving images this way. Have some fun with this process, trying not to take yourself too seriously, and see what you might discover in the process of playing. You can rest your camera on a table or an arm of a chair if you don't have a tripod. Try different angles and frames to see if one expresses something about you. Part of the discovery comes through experimentation.

Another way of approaching this weeks' theme is to look through old photos of yourself and again notice which ones stir something in you; spend time gazing upon them with the eyes of the heart. You might even scan them into your computer and play with them a little in your photo-editing software—try different ways of cropping to see what is evoked through the creation of a new frame, or play with color to increase or decrease its effect.

Remember that the self-portrait does not have to express the fullness and entire range of who you are, with all of your complexity and beauty! The idea is to capture a moment in time that reflects something about you that feels important. You may receive several images over the course of a week. Spend some time with them to notice which ones stir a stronger sense of resonance or dissonance. With self-portraits, the dissonance can be really uncomfortable but enlightening!

PHOTOGRAPHIC EXPLORATION: PERSONAL SYMBOLISM

In a sense your photographs are your autobiography.

—Dorothea Lange

Search out objects from your everyday life that are symbolic of you, not just in your most perfect moments, but in the imperfect ones as well. For example, you might include your morning cup of coffee or the vase of fresh flowers on your desk, but you might also reveal the crumpled towels in the corner, the pile of dirty dishes in the sink, laundry hanging on a line, or the rainboots left outside to dry. What calls to you for more attention? Ponder what each symbol reveals about you and how you spend your days and your lifetime. Document an ordinary sacred day. Tell your everyday story without words.

Go for a contemplative walk and seek out symbols in nature for your life right now. Notice if trees, flowers, statues, or other objects in the world speak to your life story right now.

PHOTOGRAPHIC EXPLORATION: SELF-KNOWLEDGE

How we spend our days is, of course, how we spend our lives.

—Annie Dillard

For this exploration, ponder how it is you truly spend your days. Is it on things you love, or is it on obligations and fulfilling deadlines? Do you sense something missing, or is there an experience of fullness to your time? Who are the people to whom you want to dedicate more energy? What are the dreams longing for more space? What are the *shoulds* that hang over you? Pay attention to images that reflect your false self and those that reflect your true self. What do you notice in each?

Close your eyes and go within. How are you feeling today? Try to receive that in a photograph. Pay attention to the objects around you and how they can enhance or detract from what you are trying to say.

Go on a contemplative walk, and see if you can find images that evoke a sense of your deepest dreams, longings, and wishes. Receive the images that find you.

PHOTOGRAPHIC EXPLORATION: PORTRAIT WORDS

Ask several friends to each give you two words that describe you and then make photos to represent each word. Create a photo collage of all the different images together, and see what they reveal to you about who you really are and what others see in you.

REFLECTION QUESTIONS

- What do you notice about beginning the process of receiving self-portraits? Name some of your feelings that may include hesitancy and excitement, or fear and anticipation.

- As you contemplate the theme, are there images that come immediately to mind? Pay attention to what may stir in you, and see if you can receive it without judgment. Are there new stories that have emerged during the course of this book that you would like to explore further through this theme?

- What did you discover about yourself by focusing on how your images could express something about you? Were you able to cast the loving gaze upon yourself?

8

SEEING THE HOLY EVERYWHERE

Abba Moses of Skete says: "Whenever the gaze strays even a little, we should turn back the eyes of the heart into the straight line towards [God]."

—John Cassian

If God you fail to see,
You have nothing observed.

—Angelus Silesius

Christ has no body now but yours
No hands, no feet on earth but yours
Yours are the eyes through which He looks
compassion on this world
Christ has no body now on earth but yours.

—Teresa of Avila

Images of God

In our last chapter, we began to integrate the different elements we have explored through this process. You are now invited to contemplate how God and the sacred are revealed to you through your lens. You have likely already encountered the sacred throughout your experience, but here we focus with more intention.

We have already engaged photography as a contemplative practice—slowing down, gazing with the eyes of the heart on the world, receiving (rather than taking) images as gifts, and gazing upon those images in loving, compassionate, and curious ways. In each chapter you have been invited to notice what you are discovering through the process of photography. I invite you to hold all of the threads together that you have been exploring and begin to notice if there is a larger pattern. God is present in the details of the everyday but is also visible when we pull back and take a wider gaze upon our lives and pay attention to the patterns and ways things have been woven together.

As you go out on your photographic explorations, I invite you to hold this wider perspective and longing for integration and see what is revealed to you. Carrying an awareness of shadow and light, framing, color, reflections, and your own self-image, what insights do these ways of seeing offer to you about how God is at work in the world around you? If photography is a contemplative practice, how are you being invited to see on a regular basis? How do you bring this vision to your everyday life?

Freeing Ourselves from a Too-Small God

Stillness opens the heart of the monk to a sense of wonder. When the monk is free from attachment, he or she is able to see the world apart from self-interest and self-importance. There is a willingness to look for God's presence everywhere, even in unexpected places and people.

The vulnerability of stillness becomes an environment for incarnation. The monk's soul and body are filled with an experience of God. . . . Wonder creates a mutual seeing in which the monk acknowledges the world as a gift.

—David G. R. Keller, [1]

We speak about God in images. We are creatures who understand the world through our senses, so we make sense of things through images and sensual language. No one has ever seen God; even in the story of Moses, he catches only a glimpse of God's backside. We feel God's presence at work, but the language of metaphor points to a much larger reality.

We get in trouble when we identify God solely with a narrow range of images, limiting God to only those possibilities.

In Christian spiritual tradition, there are two primary paths toward knowing God, which are to be practiced together, in tension with one another. One is the *kataphatic* way, or way of images. This is the path of sacred art and music, of guided imagination and storytelling, and of course, of photography.

The other is known as the *apophatic* way, or way of unknowing. The great mystics understood that, even when we exhaust every last image or idea of God we have, God is still much greater than all of that. God's mystery is so much more expansive than anything we can try to contain through language or art.

We need both of these paths. The kataphatic way without the apophatic becomes idolatry or the worship of images as the reality to which they point. The apophatic way without the kataphatic becomes nihilism or the belief that we can never know anything about God or even whether God exists. So they are essential to one another, and when we are exploring images, it is important to hold our grasp loosely. We run into danger when we hold too tightly onto our sacred images.

Remember Thomas Merton's photos of God I mentioned in chapter 1 of a hook hanging in the air? He did not mean that God is literally a hook but that the image evokes some of God's mystery. Consider what your own version of Merton's hook image might be.

We need to be aware of the way images of God can distort our view of ourselves and the sacred presence at the heart of the world, such as the God who tests, judges, or punishes us; the God who doles out answers to prayers as if in a divine vending machine; the God who controls everything or God whom we control; or the God who decides who is worthy of love or suffering. We all have subtle, and not so subtle, God images that are limiting.

This is the gift of photography as prayer and as a contemplative practice—to begin to see more and more the ways we limit ourselves, our vision of the world, and especially the divine presence. When we cultivate the eyes of the heart, there is more possibility, not less. We discover all the secret and subtle ways we try to confine God to certain areas of our lives, when the truth is that the holy is spilling everywhere: in the broken flower pot, in the cat missing one eye, in the dark and stormy day, in the moment of opening that comes after years of feeling suffocated, in your own beautiful heart, and in the hearts of everyone you meet.

MEDITATION: LECTIO DIVINA

Begin with a time of praying lectio divina with a scripture text. I have included several below from scripture that depict a variety of images of God. Choose one that feels unfamiliar to you, or even uncomfortable, preferably an image that you do not tend to gravitate toward. Refer back to chapter 2 for the section on lectio divina, for more background on this practice.

Enter into a time of prayer, reading the passage through twice first and listening for a word or phrase and then repeating it gently to yourself. Then read the passage again, and let the word or phrase that shimmered for you begin to unfold, paying attention to images, memories, or feelings that rise up. Sit with these for a while. Then read the passage one more time, and listen for the invitation rising up from your prayer. Close this time with silence.

Following your prayer, make some time to simply be with whatever insights came from praying with an unfamiliar image of God. Then consider going on a photo exploration to find this image in the world.

Suggested Passages

Listen to me, O house of Jacob, all the remnant of the house of Israel, who have been borne by me from your birth, carried from the womb; even to your old age I am he, even when you turn gray I will carry you. I have made, and I will bear; I will carry and will save.

—Isaiah 46:3–4

It was I who fed you in the wilderness, in the land of drought. When I fed them, they were satisfied; they were satisfied, and their heart was proud; therefore they forgot me. So I will become like a lion to them, like a leopard I will lurk beside the way. I will fall upon them like a bear robbed of her cubs, and will tear open the covering of their heart; there I will devour them like a lion, as a wild animal would mangle them.

—Hosea 13:5–8

He sustained him in a desert land, in a howling wilderness waste; he shielded him, cared for him, guarded him as the apple of his eye. As an eagle stirs up its nest, and hovers over its young; as it spreads its wings, takes them up, and bears them aloft on its pinions, the LORD alone guided him; no foreign god was with him. He set him atop the heights of the land, and fed him with produce of the field; he nursed him with honey from the crags, with oil from flinty rock;

curds from the herd, and milk from the flock, with fat of lambs and rams; Bashan bulls and goats, together with the choicest wheat—you drank fine wine from the blood of grapes.

—**Deuteronomy 32:10–14**

I am the bread of life. Your ancestors ate the manna in the wilderness, and they died. This is the bread that comes down from heaven, so that one may eat of it and not die. I am the living bread that came down from heaven. Whoever eats of this bread will live forever; and the bread that I will give for the life of the world is my flesh.

—**John 6:48–51**

When the day of Pentecost had come, they were all together in one place. And suddenly from heaven there came a sound like the rush of a violent wind, and it filled the entire house where they were sitting. Divided tongues, as of fire, appeared among them, and a tongue rested on each of them.

—**Acts 2:1–3**

PHOTOGRAPHIC EXPLORATION: SACRED IMAGES

As you engage in your contemplative walk, become aware of what is inviting you to pay attention and what you notice stirring in you in response. Receive each invitation as a gift and as a catalyst for your own reflection and inner growth. How does this image reveal new things to you, new perspectives about who God is? How might the practice of photography transform your own images of God?

Photographic Exploration: God through the Senses

As you set out on your contemplative walk, consider: What does God look like, sound like, smell like, taste like, and feel like? Keep all of your senses attuned to responses to these questions in the world around you. How might you represent these different sense experiences of the divine through imagery?

Photographic Exploration: Timeline of God Images

Spend some time in your journal contemplating all of the ways you have imagined God in your lifetime, beginning when you were very

small until now. See if you can remember as many different images as possible. Then bring your camera out into the world, and see if you discover images around you that evoke some of these. Make a series of images, and then create a sequence that tells a story about your own unfolding journey with God.

PHOTOGRAPHIC EXPLORATION: WHAT I BELIEVE

Begin by doing some free writing in response to the statement "what I believe" and then completing that phrase. Continue to do this for several minutes, each time writing a new response, digging deep inside of you to discover what values feel most important.

Then bring your camera out into the world, and see if you can receive images that speak to some of these statements of belief. Bring

them home and create another sequence; let them tell a story about your heart's commitments.

PHOTOGRAPHIC EXPLORATION: JOURNALING WITH YOUR PHOTOS

As part of your journey of integration, I invite you to go through your photos and find some that have really spoken to you—photos that have had the strongest sense of resonance or dissonance as you worked through this book. Select images that you know still have more to reveal. Print some of them out on a printer onto regular copy paper (you can use either a color or a black-and-white printer; for black-and-white printing, stronger images with contrast work best).

Take some colored pens (gel pens work especially well), and spend some time journaling right across your images. You might have your writing follow the outline of objects present in the image, or write straight across them. Listen for how you are being led. Allow this to be a time to reflect on the journey you've taken through this class, and listen for how the images are inviting you forward in your life. Engage in a free-writing process for each one, taking about ten to fifteen minutes to simply write whatever comes to mind without editing and releasing judgment. One way to begin is to ask what this image has to say to you about who God is and then dialogue right across the page. Try one or two of these each day, and see what you notice or discover.

REFLECTION QUESTIONS

- Where are the places where your image of God has grown too small for you? Where is the invitation to widen your images?

- What were you invited to notice and discover about how God is present in the world? What are the surprises?

- How do you carry this work forward with you into your daily life? How has it impacted the ways you see?

CONCLUSION

In cultivating photography as a contemplative practice, the camera becomes a tool to develop our ability to see more deeply, clearly, and truly, beneath the surface realities of the world around us and into the sacred presence shimmering in the world.

My hope is that, in exploring the language of photography, you have developed new portals into your own experience and awareness of God. Shadow and light, framing, color, reflections, and mirrors all offer us metaphors for ways of understanding how we might move toward seeing ourselves and God with the eyes of the heart.

Contemplative practice requires that we shift our normal affinity for thinking, analyzing, and producing, and surrender ourselves to a different way of being in the world, one that is more intuitive, more about mystery and unfolding rather than about planning. We follow the flow of life instead of trying to control its direction. We release our expectations of what we think we should see, and then see what is actually there. We align ourselves with a Source so much more expansive than what our own minds can imagine. Thomas Merton called it "the direct intuition of reality."

Photography as a contemplative practice means practicing seeing with the eyes of the heart. Practice is the key to developing any habit; it is the commitment of a lifetime to keep showing up. Awareness is the heart of both art and prayer. The ultimate practice is bringing this kind of vision to our everyday interaction with the world.

If you begin to notice yourself reaching for your camera to always "capture" a moment, try releasing it for a while and return again simply to the practice of sacred seeing.

> May your vision become clearer,
> may your heart become more free,
> may the eyes of your heart
> reveal the newness of the world
> at every turn.

THIS IS NOT PHOTOGRAPHY.

This is flower watching in sweet, soft September sunshine.
This is the smell of the lavender filling my senses.
This is the sound of the river rushing past, and the buzz of
the bees going mad with abundance in the herbs.
This is earth time before office time.
This is stolen time.
This is me time.
This is all time falls away and nothing else matters.
This is the way the light falls on the petals of the flower on
this softest, sweetest September morning.
This is silence.
This is all love to the flower all love from the flower.
This is being beyond thinking.
This is loving beyond judgment.
This is not photography.
This is my practice.
This is my salvation.
This is my love song.
This is my practice, and my prayer.

—**Joanna Paterson**[1]

Acknowledgments

As with every book I write, there is a whole community of people who participate in bringing it to fruition.

First and foremost is my beloved husband John who supports me every step of the way with such love and encouragement.

I am also grateful to my grandparents who encouraged their young granddaughter to explore the art of photography from an early age and gave her the tools to do so.

A deep bow of gratitude goes to each of my students who have participated in online class versions of this material, giving me an enthusiastic and receptive audience, and feedback to help me further cultivate my ideas.

I give thanks for my monastic community, the sisters of St. Placid Priory, and my fellow oblates, who support me in nurturing my contemplative vision out in the world.

And as always, to the continually receptive and enthusiastic editorial staff at Ave Maria Press, including Bob Hamma and Lil Copan who helped bring this book to publication.

NOTES

1. Seeing with Eyes of the Heart

1. Origen, quoted in Steven T. Katz, ed., *Mysticism and Sacred Scripture* (Oxford: Oxford University Press, 2000), 132.

2. St. Theophan the Recluse, quoted in Jean-Yves Leloup's *Being Still: Reflections on an Ancient Mystical Tradition*, trans. and ed. M. S. Laird (Leominster, UK: Gracewing, 2003), 124–25.

3. Kallistos Ware, "How Do We Enter the Heart?" in *Paths to the Heart: Sufism and the Christian East*, ed. James S. Cutsinger, 2–23 (Bloomington, IN: World Wisdom, 2002), 9.

4. Ibid., 8.

5. Cynthia Bourgeault, *The Wisdom Way of Knowing: Reclaiming an Ancient Tradition to Awaken the Heart* (San Francisco: Jossey-Bass, 2003), 84–85.

6. Richard Rohr, *The Naked Now: Learning to See as the Mystics See* (New York: Crossroad Publishing, 2009), 27.

7. Ibid., 28.

8. Susan Songtag, *On Photography* (New York: Picador, 2001), 9.

9. Thomas Merton, *The Road to Joy: The Letters of Thomas Merton to New and Old Friends*, selected and ed. Robert E. Daggy (San Diego: Harcourt Brace Jovanovich, 1993), March 29, 1968.

10. Thomas Merton, *A Year with Thomas Merton: Daily Meditations from His Journals*, selected and ed. Jonathan Montaldo (San Francisco: HarperSanFrancisco, 2004), 17 (January 12 and 19, 1962).

2. Practices and Tools to Cultivate Vision

1. Henry Miller, *Henry Miller on Writing* (New York: New Directions, 1964), 37.

2. Quoted in Linda Gordon, *Dorothea Lange: A Life Beyond Limits* (New York: W.W. Norton & Company, Inc., 2010), xviii.

3. The Dance of Light and Shadow

1. Henri J. M. Nouwen, *Thomas Merton: Contemplative Critic* (New York: Triumph Books, 1991).

2. Thomas Del Prete, *Thomas Merton and the Education of the Whole Person* (Birmingham, AL: Religious Education Press, 1990), 66.

3. Jalal al-Din Rumi, "Enough Words?" in *The Essential Rumi, New Expanded Edition*, trans. Coleman Barks and John Moyne (New York: HarperCollins Publishers, Inc., 2004), 20.

4. David Richo, *Shadow Dance* (Boston: Shambhala Publications, Inc., 1999), 3–5.

5. Gregory Mayers, *Listen to the Desert: Secrets of Spiritual Maturity from the Desert Fathers and Mothers* (Liguori, MO: Triumph Books, 1996), 88–89.

6. Leonard Koren, *Wabi-Sabi for Artists, Designers, Poets & Philosophers* (Point Reyes, CA: Imperfect Publishing, 2008), 7.

4. What Is Hidden and What Is Revealed?

1. Frederick Buechner, *Now and Then: A Memoir of Vocation* (New York: HarperOne, 1991), 87.

2. Mary Oliver, *New and Selected Poems, Volume One* (Boston: Beacon Press, 2005), 10.

5. The Symbolic Significance of Color

1. Oliver Davies and Thomas O'Loughlin, *Celtic Spirituality* (New York: Paulist Press, 1999), 370.

6. What Is Mirrored Back?

1. Carole Satyamurti, "Reflections" in *Stitching the Dark: New & Selected Poems* (Highgreen, England: Bloodaxe Books, 2005), 132.

2. Rumi, *The Sufi Path of Love: The Spiritual Teachings of Rumi*, trans. William C. Chittick (Albany: State University of New York Press, 1983), 162.

3. Teresa of Avila, *The Book of Her Life*, ed. Kieran Kavanaugh and Otilio Rodriguez (Indianapolis: Hackett, 2008), 304.

4. Mechthild of Magdeburg, *Selections from The Flowing Light of the Godhead*, trans. Elizabeth A. Andersen (Cambridge, UK: D. S. Brewer, 2003), 29.

7. Discovering the Holy within Us

1. Thomas Merton, *The Inner Experience: Notes on Contemplation*, ed. William H. Shannon (San Francisco: HarperSanFrancisco, 2003), 112.

2. This is an adaptation of a meditation included in Christine Valters Paintner's *Awakening the Creative Spirit: Bringing the Arts to Spiritual Direction*, coauthored with Betsey Beckman (New York: Morehouse Publishing, 2010).

8. Seeing the Holy Everywhere

1. David G. R. Keller, *Oasis of Wisdom: The Worlds of the Desert Fathers and Mothers* (Collegeville, MN: Liturgical Press, 2005), 84.

Conclusion

1. Joanna Paterson, "This Is Not Photography," accessed September 12, 2012, www.joannapaterson.co.uk/this-is-not-photography/.

Additional Resources

The Best Camera Is the One That's with You: iPhone Photography, by Chase Jarvis

A Creative Guide to Exploring Your Life: Self-Reflection Using Photography, Art, and Writing, by Graham Ramsey and Holly Sweet

The Creative Photographer, by Catherine Anderson

Exploring the Self through Photography, by Claire Craig

Expressive Photography: The Shutter Sisters Guide to Shooting from the Heart, by the Shutter Sisters

Geography of Holiness: The Photography of Thomas Merton, edited by Deba Prasad Patnaik

God Is at Eye Level, by Jan Phillips

Inner Excavation: Exploring Yourself through Photography, Poetry, and Mixed Media, by Liz Lamoreaux

The Little Book of Contemplative Photography, by Howard Zehr

Mind the Light: Learning to See with Spiritual Eyes, by J. Brent Bill

Photography and the Art of Seeing, by Freeman Patterson

Phototherapy Techniques: Exploring the Secrets of Personal Snapshots and Photo Albums, by Judy Weiser

Zen and the Magic of Photography, by Wayne Rowe

Christine Valters Paintner is the online abbess for *Abbey of the Arts,* a virtual monastery offering classes and resources on contemplative practice and creative expression. She holds a doctorate in Christian spirituality from the Graduate Theological Union in Berkeley and earned her professional status as a registered expressive arts consultant and educator from the International Expressive Arts Therapy Association. She is the author of *Water, Wind, Earth, and Fire* and *The Artist's Rule,* and is a columnist for the Progressive Christian portal at *Patheos.* She leads retreats and trains spiritual directors, living out her commitment as a Benedictine Oblate in the city of Vienna, Austria, with her husband.

Founded in 1865, Ave Maria Press,
a ministry of the Congregation of
Holy Cross, is a Catholic publishing
company that serves the spiritual and
formative needs of the Church and its
schools, institutions, and ministers;
Christian individuals and families; and
others seeking spiritual nourishment.

———————

For a complete listing of titles from

Ave Maria Press

Sorin Books

Forest of Peace

Christian Classics

visit www.avemariapress.com

ave maria press® / Notre Dame, IN 46556
A Ministry of the United States Province of Holy Cross